Writers on Writing

An anthology is like all the plums and orange peel
picked out of a cake.

Walter Alexander Raleigh (1861–1922)

Writers' & Artists'

Writers on Writing

A Book of Quotations

BLOOMSBURY YEARBOOKS
LONDON · OXFORD · NEW YORK · NEW DELHI · SYDNEY

BLOOMSBURY YEARBOOKS
Bloomsbury Publishing Plc
50 Bedford Square, London, WC1B 3DP, UK
29 Earlsfort Terrace, Dublin 2, Ireland

BLOOMSBURY, BLOOMSBURY YEARBOOKS, WRITERS' & ARTISTS'
and the Diana logo are trademarks of Bloomsbury Publishing Plc

First published in Great Britain 2021

Copyright © Bloomsbury Publishing Plc, 2021

Bloomsbury Publishing Plc does not have any control over, or responsibility for,
any third-party websites referred to or in this book. All internet addresses given
in this book were correct at the time of going to press. The author and publisher
regret any inconvenience caused if addresses have changed or sites have ceased
to exist, but can accept no responsibility for any such changes

A catalogue record for this book is available from the British Library

ISBN: HB: 978-1-4729-8697-9; eBook: 978-1-4729-8859-1

2 4 6 8 10 9 7 5 3 1

Typeset by Deanta Global Publishing Services, Chennai, India
Printed and bound in Great Britain by CPI Group (UK) Ltd, Croydon CR0 4YY

To find out more about our authors and books, visit www.bloomsbury.com
and sign up for our newsletters

Preamble

There can hardly be a stranger commodity in the world
than books. Printed by people who don't understand
them; sold by people who don't understand them; bound,
criticized and read by people who don't understand
them; and now even written by people who don't
understand them.

Georg Christoph Lichtenberg (1742–99)

The quotations in this anthology are grouped by theme,
covering aspects of the writing life, such as process and
form, genre and the characteristics and foibles of authors,
poets, agents and critics.

Where known, the original source of the quotation
or where it is quoted in a secondary work is given. At
the end of the book is a list of themes and a list of the
authors quoted.

A

Ability

It is all very well to be able to write books, but can you waggle your ears?

J. M. Barrie (1860–1937)

Said to H. G. Wells

J. A. Hammerton, *Barrie: The Story of A Genius* (1929)

We never do anything well till we cease to think about the manner of doing it.

William Hazlitt (1778–1830)

'On Prejudice', *Sketches and Essays* (1839)

There are limits to feats of skill, beyond which lie the realms of nonsense. Everything is quite difficult enough as it is, and what is simple actually comes hardest.

Hans Werner Henze (1926–2012)

Music and Politics: Collected Writings, 1953–81 (1982)

Absorption

Neglect everything else.

David Mitchell (b. 1969)

Joe Fassler, 'David Mitchell on How to Write: "Neglect Everything Else"',
The Atlantic, 23 September 2014

A

There are those great moments when you forget where you are, when you get your hands on the keys, and you don't feel anything because you're somewhere else. But that very rarely happens. Mostly I'm pounding my hands on the corpse's chest.

Mary Karr (b. 1955)
Meredith Maran (ed.), *Why We Write: 20 Acclaimed Authors on How and Why They Do What They Do* (2013)

Writing can be both addictive and unsocial!

Adele Parks (b. 1969)
Writers' & Artists' Yearbook (2011)

Achievement

To refuse awards is another way of accepting them with more noise than is normal.

Peter Ustinov (1921–2004)
'Ustinov's comic touch', BBC, 29 March 2004

Poetry is the achievement of the synthesis of hyacinths and biscuits.

Carl Sandburg (1878–1967)
'Poetry Considered', *Atlantic Monthly*, 1923

If I wanted to achieve my dream of writing for a living,
I had to believe in myself, otherwise no one else would.
Sarah Crossan (b. 1981)
Foreword to *Children's Writers' & Artists' Yearbook* (2018)

Advice

Advice is seldom welcome; and those who want it the
most always like it the least.
Lord Philip Stanhope (1694–1773)
Letter dated 29 January 1748
Letters to his Son (1774)

When we ask advice, we are usually looking for an
accomplice.
Saul Bellow (1915–2005)

Afflictions

I have a dark and dreadful secret. I write poetry...
Stephen Fry (b. 1957)
The Ode Less Travelled: Unlocking the Poet Within (2005)

To be a poet is a condition rather than a profession.
Robert Graves (1895–1985)
'The Cost of Letters', *Horizon* (1946)

Age

The trouble with our younger authors is that they are all in their sixties.

W. Somerset Maugham (1874–1965)
Observer, 17 October 1951

A budding young anthologist sought to include a Shaw piece in a new collection. "I hope you understand", he wrote to Shaw, "that I cannot afford to pay your usual fee as I am a very young man." Shaw replied, "I'll wait for you to grow up."

Bennett Cerf (1898–1971)
Shake Well Before Using (1950)

When I was a little boy they called me a liar but now that I am a grown up they call me a writer.

Neil Simon (1927–2018)
The Times, 4 August 1990

Most poets are dead by their late twenties.

Robert Graves (1895–1985)
Observer, 11 November 1962

Agents

That's the only general advice I ever feel comfortable giving about agents — that I think the language of love can be a shared language that can help show a writer where to go next and whom they might want to work with.

R. O. Kwon
'How These Writers Got a Literary Agent', *The Cut*, 24 July 2020

It is easier for an unpublished writer to find a needle in a haystack than an agent. And easier for a camel to pass through the eye of that needle than for an unagented writer to find a publisher.

Lawrence Norfolk (b. 1963)
Foreword to *Writers' & Artists' Yearbook* (2012)

Alcohol

It has become increasingly plain to me that the very excellent organisation of a long book or the finest perceptions and judgment in time of revision do not go well with liquor.

F. Scott Fitzgerald (1896–1940)
Letter to his editor Maxwell Perkins in 1933
Quoted in Travis Elborough & Helen Gordon, *Being a Writer* (2017)

A

So, How do we get through this puzzle? That's funny,
I thought I could write this book and I can't, instead of,
I have to drink a bottle of gin before 11:00 to numb myself
at how horrifying this is.

Elizabeth Gilbert (b. 1969)

Joe Fassler, 'The "Stubborn Gladness" of Elizabeth Gilbert's Favorite Poet',
The Atlantic, 6 November 2013

Language is wine upon the lips.

Virginia Woolf (1882–1941)

[...] the passion for good wine and good writing is not so
different. It's always about a great story.

Nina Caplan

'My Cup Runneth Over', *Harper's Bazaar*, March 2018

No alcohol, sex or drugs while you are working.

Colm Tóibín (b. 1955)

'Ten rules for writing fiction (Part two)', the *Guardian*, 20 February 2010

Ambition

I want to look like an American Voltaire or Gibbon,
but am slowly settling down to be a third-rate Boswell
hunting for a Dr. Johnson.

Henry Adams (1838–1918)

Ernest Samuels, *Henry Adams: The Major Phase* (1965)

When I was little, my ambition was to grow up to be a book.

Amos Oz (1939–2018)
A Tale of Love and Darkness (2004)

I shall not be satisfied unless I produce something that shall for a few days supersede the last fashionable novel on the tables of young ladies.

Thomas Babington Macaulay (1800–59)
Letter to Macvey Napier, 5 November 1841

An artist cannot do anything slovenly.

Jane Austen (1775–1817)
Letter to her sister Cassandra, 1798

Animals

You might not think that these two interests, capturing animals and writing poems, have much in common. But the more I think back the more sure I am that with me the two interests have been one interest.

Ted Hughes (1930–98)
Poetry in the Making (1967)

Poetry is always the cat concert under the window of the room in which the official version of reality is being written.

Charles Simic (b. 1938)
Quoted in Harold Bloom (ed.), *The Best of the Best American Poetry 1988-1997* (1998)

English literature's performing flea.

Sean O'Casey (1880–1964)
Referring to P. G. Wodehouse

Insects sting, not from malice, but because they want to live. It is the same with critics—they desire our blood, not our pain.

Friedrich Wilhelm Nietzsche (1844–1900)
Assorted Opinions and Maxims (1879)

Anxiety

Fear is felt by writers at every level. Anxiety accompanies the first word they put on paper and the last.

Ralph Keyes (b. 1945)
The Courage to Write: How Writers Transcend Fear (1995)

We're professional worriers. You're constantly imagining things that could go wrong and then writing about them.

John Green (b. 1977)
The Late Late Show with Craig Ferguson, CBS, 19 March 2013

Attention

I could answer that a writer is someone who pays attention to the world.

Susan Sontag (1933–2004)
Edward Hirsch, 'Susan Sontag, The Art of Fiction No. 143', *The Paris Review*, Winter 1995

Due attention to the inside of books, and due contempt for the outside, is the proper relation between a man of sense and his books.

Lord Philip Stanhope (1694–1773)
Letters to his Son, 10 January 1749

Your manuscript is your baby, maybe your only child, but the publisher finds a dozen or so new babies on his doorstep every morning and has several thousand older children over-running his warehouse and his entire establishment, all of them calling simultaneously for his undivided attention.

Stanley Unwin (1884–1968)
Writers' & Artists' Yearbook (1950)

Audience

Literature is also, a curiously intimate way of communicating with people whom you will never meet.

Julian Barnes (b. 1946)

Shusha Guppy, 'Julian Barnes, The Art of Fiction No. 165', *The Paris Review*, Winter 2000

In play writing, as distinct from any other sort of writing, the author must continually see his work through the eyes of the audience.

A. A. Milne (1882–1956)

Writers' & Artists' Yearbook (1933)

You're allowed to bore your friends and family, but to bore your audience is unforgivable.

Phoebe Waller-Bridge (b. 1985)

Gaby Wood, 'Phoebe Waller-Bridge Shocked and Delighted With *Fleabag*. What Comes Next?', *Vogue*, November 2017

[…] the communal nature of the audience is like having five hundred people read your novel and respond to it at the same time.

August Wilson (1945–2005)

Bonnie Lyons & George Plimpton, 'August Wilson, The Art of Theater No. 14', *The Paris Review*, Winter 1999

I NEVER DELIBERATELY SET OUT TO SHOCK, BUT WHEN PEOPLE DON'T WALK OUT OF MY PLAYS I THINK THERE IS SOMETHING WRONG.

John Osborne (1929–94)
'Sayings of the Week', *Observer*, 19 January 1975

———————————

THE PLAY WAS A GREAT SUCCESS, BUT THE AUDIENCE WAS A DISASTER.

Oscar Wilde (1854–1900)

———————————

A

If by the people you understand the multitude, the *hoi polloi*, 'tis no matter what they think; they are sometimes in the right, sometimes in the wrong; their judgement is a mere lottery.

John Dryden (1631–1700)
Essay of Dramatick Poesie (1688)

Some writers take to drink, others take to audiences.

Gore Vidal (1925–2012)
The Paris Review, 1981

Authenticity

Things are entirely what they appear to be and *behind them*...there is nothing.

Jean-Paul Sartre (1905–80)
Nausea (1963)

But above all, in order to be, never try to seem.

Albert Camus (1913–60)
Notebooks 1935–1951

Some writers confuse authenticity, which they ought always to aim at, with originality, which they should never bother about.

W. H. Auden (1907–73)
The Dyer's Hand (1962)

[I] will not have in my writing any elegance, or effect or originality—to hang in the way between me and the rest like curtains...What I tell I tell for precisely what it is.

Walt Whitman (1819–92)
'Preface', *Leaves of Grass* (1855)

But if you wanted to know what the retreat from Moscow really felt like, you wouldn't read a history of the Napoleonic wars—you'd read *War and Peace*.

Joanna Trollope (b. 1943)
Claire Armistead, 'Joanna Trollope on families, fiction and feminism: "Society still expects women to do all the caring", the *Guardian*, 2 March 2020

Autobiography

An autobiography is an obituary in serial form with the last instalment missing.

Quentin Crisp (1908–99)
The Naked Civil Servant (1968)

Language is the autobiography of the human mind.

Max Müller (1823–1900)
Nirad C. Chaudhuri (ed.), *Scholar Extraordinary* (1974)

Every artist writes his own autobiography.

Havelock Ellis (1859–1939)
'Tolstoy', *The New Spirit* (1890)

THERE IS BAD IN ALL GOOD AUTHORS: WHAT A PITY THE CONVERSE ISN'T TRUE!

Philip Larkin (1922–85)

Anthony Thwaite (ed.), *Philip Larkin: Letters to Monica* (2011)

———————————

CHOOSE AN AUTHOR AS YOU CHOOSE A FRIEND.

Wentworth Dillon (c.1637–85)

Essay on Translated Verse (1684)

———————————

[...] remember that in the particularity of your own life lies the seedcorn that will feed your imaginative work. So don't throw it all away on autobiography. (There are quite enough writers' memoirs out there already.)

Rose Tremain (b. 1943)

'Ten rules for writing fiction (Part two)', the *Guardian*, 20 February 2010

All those writers who write about their own childhood! Gentle God, if I wrote about mine you wouldn't sit in the same room with me.

Dorothy Parker (1893–1967)

Marion Capron, 'Dorothy Parker, The Art of Fiction No. 13', *The Paris Review*, Summer 1956

B

Bad writing

Read widely and with discrimination. Bad writing is contagious.

P. D. James (1920–2014)

'Ten rules for writing fiction', the *Guardian*, 20 February 2010

One should accept bad writing as a way of priming the pump, a warm-up exercise that allows you to write well.

Jennifer Egan (b. 1962)

Meredith Maran (ed.), *In Why We Write: 20 Acclaimed Authors on How and Why They Do What They Do* (2013)

Don't hold on to poor work. If it was bad when it went in the drawer it will be just as bad when it comes out.

Jeanette Winterson (b. 1959)

'Ten rules for writing fiction', the *Guardian*, 20 February 2010

It takes a lot of bad writing to get to a little good writing.

Truman Capote (1924–84)

'Folly and Female Education', *What's Wrong with the World* (1912)

Becoming a writer

I became a writer the way other people become monks or nuns.

Elizabeth Gilbert (b. 1969)

'Thoughts on Writing', www.elizabethgilbert.com/thoughts-on-writing/

B

But it is when we have a story beating wildly deep inside in the chambers of our hearts, making us lose sleep at nights, asking to be born, demanding to be told, clawing at our flesh, a story stronger and wiser and ultimately better than our deeply flawed selves, that is when we start to become a writer.

Elif Shafak (b. 1971)
'Elif Shafak on Becoming a Writer', *Waterstones Blog*, 28 August 2020

Becoming a writer is not a 'career decision' like becoming a doctor or a policeman. You don't choose it so much as get chosen, and you have to be prepared to walk a long, hard road for the rest of your days.

Paul Auster (b. 1947)
Hand to Mouth (1997)

I believe writers are writers the day they describe themselves as such.

Adele Parks (b. 1969)
Writers' & Artists' Yearbook (2011)

Beginnings

For a true writer each book should be a new beginning where he tries again for something that is beyond attainment.

Ernest Hemingway (1899–1961)
Acceptance speech, Nobel Prize in Literature, 1954

There is something delicious about writing the first words
of a story. You never quite know where they'll take you.

Beatrix Potter (1866–1943)

There is an old saying 'well begun is half done'—'tis a bad
one. I would use instead—Not begun at all 'til half done.

John Keats (1795–1821)

Letter to Benjamin Robert Haydon, 10–11 May 1817

Robert Gittings (ed.), *Letters of John Keats* (1970)

Never begin the book when you feel you want to begin it,
but hold off a while longer.

Rose Tremain (b. 1943)

'Ten rules for writing fiction (Part two)', the *Guardian*, 20 February 2010

The last thing one knows in constructing a work is what
to put first.

Blaise Pascal (1623–62)

Pensées (1670)

Bestseller

A best-seller is the gilded tomb of a mediocre talent.

Logan Pearsall Smith (1865–1946)

'Arts and Letters', *Afterthoughts* (1931)

B

How long most people would look at the best book before they would give the price of a large turbot for it?

John Ruskin (1819–1900)
'Of Kings' Treasuries', *Sesame and Lilies* (1865)

Biography

The Art of Biography
Is different from Geography.
Geography is about Maps,
But Biography is about Chaps.

Edmund Clerihew Bentley (1875–1956)
Biography for Beginners (1925)

A well-written life is almost as rare as a well-spent one.

Thomas Carlyle (1795–1881)
'Jean Paul Friedrich Richter', *Edinburgh Review*, June 1827

Shakespeare is the only biographer of Shakespeare; and even he can tell nothing, except to the Shakespeare in us; that is, to our most apprehensive and sympathetic hour.

Ralph Waldo Emerson (1803–82)
'Shakespeare; or the Poet', *Representative Men* (1850)

I have a certain hesitation in starting my biography too soon for fear of something important having not yet happened.

Bertrand Russell (1872–1970)

Letter to Stanley Unwin, November 1930

If you have to read, to cheer yourself up read biographies of writers who went insane.

Colm Tóibín (b. 1955)

'Ten rules for writing fiction (Part two)', the *Guardian*, 20 February 2010

Just how difficult it is to write biography can be reckoned by anybody who sits down and considers just how many people know the real truth about his or her love affairs.

Rebecca West (1892–1983)

Vogue (1952)

Birds

Her prose is like a bird darting from place to place, palpitating with nervous energy; but a bird with a bright beady eye and a sharp beak as well.

Francis Hope (1938–1974)

About Muriel Spark
Observer, 28 April 1963

B

All my novels are an accumulation of detail. I'm a bit of a bower-bird.

Patrick White (1912–90)

'A Conversation with Patrick White', *Southerly*, Vol. 3, Issue 2, 1973

Birth

To animate, in the precise sense of the word: to give life to.

Federico García Lorca (1898–1936)

Inaugural lecture for the Granada Athenæum Theatre's season
Leslie Stainton, *Lorca: A Dream of Life* (1999)

Poetry is the voice of a poet at its birth, the voice of a people in its ultimate fulfilment as a successful and useful work of art.

Guy Davenport (1927–2005)

The Geography of the Imagination (1981)

I wasn't born until I started to write.

David Hare (b. 1947)

Sunday Times, 11 February 1990

I get an urge, like a pregnant elephant, to go away and give birth to a book.

Stephen Fry (b. 1957)

Books

Few books today are forgivable.
R. D. Laing (1927–89)
The Politics of Experience (1967)

The proper study of mankind is books.
Aldous Huxley (1894–1963)
Crome Yellow (1921)

Books create eras and nations, just as eras and nations create books.
Jean-Jaques Ampère (1800–64)
Mélanges d'histoire littéraire et de littérature (1876)

Some books are undeservedly forgotten; none are undeservedly remembered.
W. H. Auden (1907–73)
'Reading', *The Dyer's Hand* (1963)

Some books are to be tasted, others to be swallowed, and some few to be chewed and digested.
Francis Bacon (1561–1626)
Michael J. Hawkins (ed.), 'Of Studies', *Essays (1625)* (1973)

Take a good book to bed with you—books don't snore.
Thea Dorn (b. 1970)

A BOOK IS NOT HARMLESS MERELY BECAUSE NO ONE IS CONSCIOUSLY OFFENDED BY IT.

T. S. Eliot (1888–1965)

'Religion and Literature', *T.S. Eliot Selected Essays* (1932)

Books are made not like children but like pyramids...and they're just as useless! and they stay in the desert!...Jackals piss at their foot and the bourgeois climb up on them.

Gustave Flaubert (1821–80)

Letter to Ernest Feydeau, November/December 1857

The possession of a book becomes a substitute for reading it.

Anthony Burgess (1917–93)

New York Times Book Review (1966)

The age of the book is almost gone.

George Steiner (1929–2020)

Daily Mail, 27 June 1988

Bookshelf

The answers to a lot of aspiring writers' problems are as close as the bookshelf. Use it.

Bernard Cornwell (b. 1944)

Writers' & Artists' Yearbook (2006)

No furniture so charming as books.

Sydney Smith (1771–1845)

Lady Holland, *A Memoir of the Rev. Sydney Smith* (1855)

B

Boredom

I've got a great ambition to die of exhaustion rather than
boredom.
Thomas Carlyle (1795–1881)

Punctuality is the virtue of the bored.
Evelyn Waugh (1903–66)
Diary entry, 26 March 1962
Michael Davie (ed.), 'Irregular Notes', *Diaries of Evelyn Waugh* (1976)

Brevity

Not that the story need be long, but it will take a long
while to make it short.
Henry David Thoreau (1817–62)
Letter to Harrison Blake, 16 November 1857

In art economy is always beauty.
Henry James (1843–1916)
'Preface', *The Altar of the Dead* (1909)

There are writers who can express in as little as twenty
pages what I occasionally need as many as two for.
Karl Kraus (1874–1936)
Harry Zohn (ed.), *Half-Truths and One-And-A-Half-Truths: Selected Aphorisms*
(1990)

REMEMBER WRITING DOESN'T LOVE YOU. IT DOESN'T CARE. NEVERTHELESS, IT CAN BEHAVE WITH REMARKABLE GENEROSITY. SPEAK WELL OF IT, ENCOURAGE OTHERS, PASS IT ON.

A. L. Kennedy (b. 1965)

'Ten rules for writing fiction', the *Guardian*, 20 February 2010

C

Career

A professional writer is an amateur who didn't quit.
   Richard Bach (b. 1936)

So I had this problem—work or starve. So I thought I'd combine the two and decided to become a writer.
   Robert Bloch (1917–94)

I wanted to use what I was, to be what I was born to be—not to have a 'career', but to be that straightforward obvious unmistakable animal, a writer.
   Cynthia Ozick (b. 1928)
   Metaphor and Memory (1989)

Characters

In the novel as in literature as a whole, the problem is how to invent; above all how to invent characters who have life.
   Pío Baroja (1872–1956)
   Derek Harris, *The Spanish Avant-Garde* (1995)

You can't blame a writer for what the characters say.
   Truman Capote (1924–84)

C

If you get the landscape right, the characters will step out of it, and they'll be in the right place.

E. Annie Proulx (b. 1935)

Time, 29 November 1993

If you live long enough you see so much—sometimes things you think you can't manage. And in fiction they pass through a kind of sieve, which is the consciousness of a character.

Meg Wolitzer (b. 1959)

Erica Wagner, 'The Crest of a Wave', *Harper's Bazaar*, July 2018

You need to form a double act with the author. The author is the main character though; as an illustrator, you have to play up to them.

Quentin Blake (b. 1932)

'Interview with Quentin Blake', British Library, 21 February 2020

Children

An author who speaks about his own books is almost as bad as a mother who talks about her own children.

Benjamin Disraeli (1804–81)

Speech at a banquet held in Glasgow for his installation as Lord Rector

The Times, 20 November 1873

You must write for children in the same way as you do for adults, only better.
   Maksim Gorky (1868–1936)

Authors are easy to get on with—if you're fond of children.
   Michael Joseph (1897–1958)
   Observer, 1949

A children's story that can only be enjoyed by children is not a good children's story in the slightest.
   C. S. Lewis (1893–1963)

It is healthier, in any case, to write for the adults one's children will become than for the children one's 'mature' critics often are.
   Alice Walker (b. 1944)
   'A Writer, Because of, Not in Spite of, Her Children', *Ms*, January 1979

Clarity

Clarity is the politeness of the man of letters.
   Jules Renard (1864–1910)
   Journal, 1887–1910 (1925)

C

We should constantly use the most common, little, easy words (so they are pure and proper) which our language affords.
> **John Wesley** (1703–91)
> *Wesley's Works*, Vol. 8 (1764)

The great enemy of clear language is insincerity. When there is a gap between one's real and one's declared aims, one turns as it were instinctively to long words and exhausted idioms, like a cuttlefish squirting out ink.
> **George Orwell** (1903–1950)
> 'Politics and the English Language', *Shooting an Elephant and Other Essays* (1950)

A Classic

The book, when it came out in 1965, was considered an instant classic, largely because Capote told everyone it was.
> **Bill Bryson** (b. 1951)
> Referring to Truman Capote's *In Cold Blood* (1965)
> *The Lost Continent* (1989)

A classic book is a book that survives the circumstances that made it possible yet alone keeps those circumstances alive.
> **Alfred Kazin** (1915–98)
> Quoted in *The New Republic*, 29 August 1988

Clichés

The cliché is dead poetry. English, being the language of an imaginative race, abounds in clichés, so that English literature is always in danger of being poisoned by its own secretions.
Gerald Brenan (1894–1987)
'Literature', *Thoughts in a Dry Season* (1978)

Drop 30 per cent of your Latinisms...mow down every old cliché, uproot all the dragging circumlocutions, compress, diversify, clarify, vivify, & you'll make a book that will be read and talked of.
Edith Wharton (1862–1937)
Letter to W. Morton Fullerton, 24 March 1910
R. W. B. Lewis and Nancy Lewis (eds), *The Letters of Edith Wharton* (1988)

But I cannot abide Conrad's souvenir-shop style, and bottled ships, and shell necklaces of romanticist clichés.
Vladimir Nabokov (1899–1977)
Alvin Toffler, 'Playboy interview: Vladimir Nabokov', *Playboy*, January 1964

The first man who compared woman to a rose was a poet, the second, an imbecile.
Gerard de Naval (1808–1955)

Comfort

Poetry is the revelation of a feeling that the poet believes to be interior and personal but which the reader recognizes as his own.

Salvatore Quasimodo (1901–68)
New York Times, 14 May 1960

Poetry is the record of the best and happiest moments of the happiest and best minds.

Percy Bysshe Shelley (1792–1822)
Mary Shelley (ed.), *Essays, Letters from Abroad, Translations and Fragments* (1940)

The human creature is alone in his carapace. Poetry is a strong way out.

Stevie Smith (1902–71)
'My Muse', *Selected Poems* (1962)

I had a teacher I liked who used to say good fiction's job was to comfort the disturbed and disturb the comfortable.

David Foster Wallace (1962–2008)
Larry McCaffery, 'An Interview with David Foster Wallace', *Review of Contemporary Fiction*, Summer 1993

Communication

Words are the tokens current and accepted for conceits, as moneys are for values.
Francis Bacon (1561–1626)
The Advancement of Learning (1605)

It is generally better to deal by speech than by letter.
Francis Bacon (1561–1626)
'Of Negotiating', *Essays* (1625)

In communications, familiarity breeds apathy.
William Bernbach (1911–82)
Bill Bernbach Said... (1989)

Online conversation is...talking by writing.
John Coate (b. 1951)
Philip E. Agre & Douglas Schuler (eds), 'Cyberspace Innkeeping', *Reinventing Technology, Rediscovering Community* (1997)

Don't you like writing letters? I do because it's such a swell way to keep from working and yet feel you've done something.
Ernest Hemingway (1899–1961)
Letter to F. Scott Fitzgerald, 1 July 1925

C

It is better not to express what one means than to express what one does not mean.

Karl Kraus (1874–1936)

Harry Zohn (ed. and trans.), *In These Great Times: A Karl Kraus Reader* (1984)

Complaints

Never complain of being misunderstood. You can choose to be understood, or you can choose not to.

David Hare (b. 1947)

'Ten rules for writing fiction', the *Guardian*, 20 February 2010

I have always been a grumbler. I am designed for the part—sagging face, weighty underlip, rumbling, resonant voice. Money couldn't buy a better grumbling outfit.

J. B. Priestley (1894–1984)

The *Guardian*, 15 August 1984

Conceit

Only the insane take themselves quite seriously.

Max Beerbohm (1872–1956)

D. Cecil, *Max: A Biography* (1964)

Conceit is the finest armour a man can wear.

Jerome K. Jerome (1859–1927)

Idle Thoughts of an Idle Fellow (1886)

Confidence

I've never waited for the confidence to do anything, because if I was waiting for confidence, I would still be waiting.

Roxane Gay (b. 1974)

Micha Frazer-Carroll, 'Roxane Gay: "If I was waiting for confidence to write, I'd still be waiting"', *gal-dem*, 15 January 2019

Those who believe that they are exclusively in the right are generally those who achieve something.

Aldous Huxley (1894–1963)

Proper Studies (1927)

If I ever felt inclined to be timid as I was going into a room full of people, I would say to myself, 'You're the cleverest member of one of the cleverest families in the cleverest class of the cleverest nation in the world, why should you be frightened?'

Beatrice Webb (1858–1943)

Quoted in Bertrand Russell, *Portraits from Memory* (1956)

C

I think I shall be among the English Poets after my death.
   John Keats (1795–1821)
   Letter to George and Georgiana Keats, 14 October 1818
   H. E. Rollins (ed.), *Letters of John Keats, Vol. 2* (1958)

Conversation

If you haven't anything nice to say about anyone, come
and sit by me.
   Alice Lee Longworth (1884–1980)
   Time, 9 December 1966

There is only one rule for being a good talker—learn to
listen.
   Christopher Darlington Morley (1890–1957)

Beware of the conversationalist who adds 'in other words'.
He is merely starting afresh.
   Robert Morley (1908–92)
   'Sayings of the Week', *Observer*, 6 December 1964

Reading is a conversation. All books talk. But a good
book listens as well.
   Mark Haddon (b. 1962)
   'B is for bestseller', the *Guardian*, 11 April 2004

Ideal conversation must be an exchange of thought, and not, as many of those who worry most about their shortcomings believe, an eloquent exhibition of wit or oratory.

Emily Post (1872–1960)
Etiquette: The Blue Book of Social Usage (1922)

He has occasional flashes of silence, that make his conversation perfectly delightful.

Sydney Smith (1771–1845)
Referring to Lord Macaulay
Lady Holland, *A Memoir of the Rev. Sydney Smith* (1855)

The arts babblative and scribblative.

Robert Southey (1774–1843)
Tom Duggett (ed.), *Sir Thomas More: or, Colloquies on the Progress and Prospects of Society* (2017)

A good listener is not someone who has nothing to say. A good listener is a good talker with a sore throat.

Katharine Whitehorn (1928–2021)

I like plays where people talk a lot. Conversation is sustained. Argument is sustained.

Tom Stoppard (b. 1937)
David Cote, 'Tom Stoppard interview: "I've always been strangely eclectic"', timeout.com, 17 September 2014

NEVER JUDGE A COVER BY ITS BOOK.

Fran Lebowitz (b. 1950)
Metropolitan Life (1978)

———————————

CRAMMING AS MUCH OF NEW YORK CITY BETWEEN THE COVERS AS YOU COULD, WAS THE MOST TEMPTING, THE MOST CHALLENGING, AND THE MOST OBVIOUS IDEA THAT AN AMERICAN WRITER COULD POSSIBLY HAVE.

Tom Wolfe (1930–2018)
Harper's, November 1989

———————————

Creativity

A creative life is more of a scavenger hunt, following a trail of breadcrumbs than it is lightning in a bottle.
Elizabeth Gilbert (b. 1969)
Brooke Warner, 'My Interview with Liz Gilbert (on Big Magic, Permission, Authority, Her Facebook Group, and More)', *SheWrites*, October 2015

I am always half where I am; the other half is feeding the furnace, kick-starting the heat of creativity. I am making love with someone but at the same time I'm noticing how this graceful hand across my belly might just fit in with the memory of lilacs in Albuquerque in 1974.
Natalie Goldberg (b. 1948)
Thunder and Lightning: Cracking Open the Writer's Craft (2000)

There's no point in trying to analyse the creative urge. You either have it or you don't.
David Hewson (b. 1953)
Writing: A User Manual (2012)

The worst enemy to creativity is self-doubt.
Sylvia Plath (1932–63)
Karen V. Kukil (ed.), *The Unabridged Journals of Sylvia Plath, 1950–1962* (2000)

Criticism

I am bound by my own definition of criticism: a disinterested endeavour to learn and propagate the best that is known and thought in the world.

Matthew Arnold (1822–88)
'Functions of Criticism at the Present Time', *Essays in Criticism, First Series* (1865)

A great deal of contemporary criticism reads to me like a man saying: 'Of course I do not like green cheese: I am very fond of brown sherry.'

G. K. Chesterton (1874–1936)
'On Jonathan Swift', *All I Survey* (1933)

Last year it was all Sean O'Casey: now it is all shun O'Casey.

Joseph Holloway (1861–1944)
Impressions of a Dublin Playgoer, 30 August 1926

All of us, readers and writers, are bereft when criticism remains too polite or too fearful to notice a disrupting darkness before its eyes.

Toni Morrison (1931–2019)
Playing in the Dark: Whiteness and the Literary Imagination (1992)

Re-vision—the act of looking back, of seeing with fresh eyes, of entering an old text from a new critical direction—is for women more than a chapter in cultural history: it is an act of survival.
Adrienne Rich (1929–2012)
'When We Dead Awaken', *On Lies, Secrets, and Silence* (1979)

It had only one fault. It was kind of lousy.
James Thurber (1894–1961)

I never read anything concerning my work. I feel that criticism is a letter to the public which the author, since it is not directed to him, does not have to open and read.
Rainer Maria Rilke (1875–1926)
Letters of Rainer Maria Rilke (1945)

Writing criticism is to writing fiction and poetry as hugging the shore is to sailing the open sea.
John Updike (1932–2009)
'Foreword', *Hugging the Shore* (1983)

As far as criticism is concerned, we don't resent that unless it is absolutely biased, as it is in most cases.
John Vorster (1915–83)
'Sayings of the Week', *Observer*, 9 November 1969

Reading Proust is like bathing in someone else's dirty water.

Alexander Woollcott (1887–1943)

Critics

A critic is a bunch of biases held loosely together by a sense of taste.

Whitney Balliett (1926–2007)
Dinosaurs in the Morning (1962)

Critics!—appall'd I venture on the name,
Those cut-throat bandits in the paths of fame.

Robert Burns (1759–96)
CXXVII. to Robert Graham, Esq., of Fintry (1791)

Never trust the artist. Trust the tale. The proper function of a critic is to save the tale from the artist who created it.

D. H. Lawrence (1885–1930)
Studies in Classic American Literature (1923)

If I had listened to the critics I'd have died drunk in the gutter.

Anton Chekhov (1860–1904)
Quoted in Arthur Miller, *Timebends* (1999)

The critic is...the younger brother of genius. Next to invention is the power of interpreting invention; next to beauty the power of appreciating beauty...The critic, then, should be not merely a poet, not merely a philosopher, not merely an observer, but tempered of all three.

Margaret Fuller (1810–50)

Paul Lauter (ed.), *The Heath Anthology of American Literature* (1989)

Remember: when people tell you something's wrong or doesn't work for them, they are almost always right. When they tell you exactly what they think is wrong and how to fix it, they are almost always wrong.

Neil Gaiman (b. 1960)

'Ten rules for writing fiction', the *Guardian*, 20 February 2010

A drama critic is a person who surprises the playwright by informing him what he meant.

Wilson Mizner (1876–1933)

Critics are more malicious about poetry than about other books—maybe because so many manqué poets write reviews.

Elizabeth Jennings (1926–2001)

Remark made in December 1987

C

A critic should be a conduit, a bridge, but not a law.
Toni Morrison (1931–2019)
'Interview', Black Creation Annual 1974–1975

The greater part of critics are parasites, who, if nothing
had been written, would find nothing to write.
J. B. Priestley (1894–1984)
Outcries and Asides (1974)

A critic is a man who knows the way but can't drive
the car.
Kenneth Tynan (1927–80)
New York Times Magazine, 9 January 1966

Cynicism

Youthful cynicism is sad to observe, because it indicates
not so much knowledge learned from bitter experiences as
insufficient trust even to attempt the future.
Maya Angelou (1928–2014)
The Heart of a Woman (1981)

When morality comes up against profit, it is seldom that
profit loses.
Shirley Chisholm (1924–2005)
Unbought and Unbossed (1970)

There is no such thing on earth as an uninteresting subject; the only thing that can exist is an uninterested person.

G. K. Chesterton (1874–1936)
Heretics (1905)

I've always been interested in people, but I've never liked them.

W. Somerset Maugham (1874–1965)
'Sayings of the Week', *Observer*, 28 August 1949

A cynic is a man who, when he smells flowers, looks around for a coffin.

H. L. Mencken (1880–1956)

The worst cynicism: a belief in luck.

Joyce Carol Oates (b. 1938)

D

Death

This pretense that it's happening now is a silly thing which I can't abide, and I use every opportunity to bore people to death by telling them about it.
Philip Pullman (b. 1946)
Alexandra Schwartz, 'The Fallen Worlds of Philip Pullman', *The New Yorker*, 29 September 2019

Sometimes part of a book simply gets up and walks away. The writer cannot force it back into place. It wanders off to die.
Annie Dillard (b. 1945)
The Writing Life (1989)

I am a deceased writer not in the sense of one who has written and is now deceased, but in the sense of one who has died and is now writing.
Joaquim Maria Machado de Assis (1839–1908)
Epitaph of a Small Winner (1880)

I think it's good for a writer to think he's dying; he works harder.
Tennessee Williams (1911–83)
'Sayings of the Week', *Observer*, 31 October 1976

It was a book to kill time for those who like it better dead.
Rose Macaulay (1881–1958)

Discipline

No one asked you to be happy. Get to work.
Colette (1873–1954)

A work in progress quickly becomes feral. It reverts to a wild state overnight. […] You must visit it every day and reassert your mastery over it.
Annie Dillard (b. 1945)
The Writing Life (1989)

The road to hell is paved with works-in-progress.
Philip Roth (1933–2018)
New York Times Book Review, 15 July 1979

Sit myself in my chair and threaten myself like a recalcitrant child: you will sit in this chair and you will not move until you get this scene written, missy.
Gillian Flynn (b. 1971)
Noah Charney, 'Gillian Flynn: How I Write', *The Daily Beast*, 14 July 2017

Dislikes

There are two ways of disliking poetry; one way is to dislike it, the other is to read Pope.

Oscar Wilde (1854–1900)

I'm also a believer in reading what you dislike at least once, just to know.

Chimamanda Ngozi Adichie (b. 1977)

Susan VanZanten, 'A Conversation with Chimamanda Ngozi Adichie', *Image*, Issue 65

Try to avoid asking a writer who's a woman any question that starts 'As a woman...'

Emma Donoghue (b. 1969)

'An Exclusive Interview with Emma Donoghue', *SheWrites*, 24 September 2019

I dislike Allegory—the conscious and intentional allegory—yet any attempt to explain the purport of myth or fairytale must use allegorical language.

J. R. R. Tolkien (1916–71)

In a letter to Milton Waldman, 1951

D

Dogs

If you write about a dog, and the dog dies, you are in trouble.

Matt Haig (b. 1975)
'25 rules for writing a novel', *BookTrust*

Outside of a dog, a book is a man's best friend. Inside of a dog, it's too hard to read.

Groucho Marx (1890–1977)

Asking a working writer what he thinks about critics is like asking a lamp-post how it feels about dogs.

Christopher Hampton (b. 1946)
Time Magazine, 16 October 1977

Dullness

What have I gained by health? intolerable dullness. What by early hours and moderate meals?—a total blank.

Charles Lamb (1775–1834)
Letter to William Wordsworth, 22 January 1830

He was dull in a new way, and that made many people think him *great*.

Samuel Johnson (1709–84)

James Boswell, *Life of Samuel Johnson* (1791)

A book is like a man—clever and dull, brave and cowardly, beautiful and ugly. For every flowering thought there will be a page like a wet and mangy mongrel, and for every looping flight a tap on the wing and a reminder that wax cannot hold the feathers firm too near the sun.

John Steinbeck (1902–68)

Journal of a novel: The East of Eden Letters (1968)

Editing

It was like removing layers of crumpled brown paper from an awkwardly shaped parcel, and revealing the attractive present which it contained.

Diana Athill (1917–2019)

Stet: An Editor's Life (2000)

I may write garbage, but you can always edit garbage. You can't edit a blank page.

Jodi Picoult (b. 1966)

Melody Joy Kramer, 'Jodi Picoult: You Can't Edit a Blank Page', *NPR*, 22 November 2006

Fiction happens in the womb. It doesn't get processed in the mind until you do the editing.

Isabel Allende (b. 1942)

Meredith Maran (ed.), *In Why We Write: 20 Acclaimed Authors on How and Why They Do What They Do* (2013)

Substitute 'damn' every time you're inclined to write 'very'; your editor will delete it and the writing will be just as it should be.

Mark Twain (1835–1910)

Kate Kiefer Lee, 'Mark Twain On Writing: "Kill Your Adjectives"', *Forbes*, 30 November 2012

Read over your compositions, and where ever you meet with a passage which you think is particularly fine, strike it out.

Samuel Johnson (1709–84)

James Boswell, *Life of Samuel Johnson* (1992)

Editors

Where were you fellows when the paper was blank?

Fred Allen (1894–1956)

Remark to writers who heavily edited one of his scripts

Some editors are failed writers, but so are most writers.

T. S. Eliot (1888–1965)

Allen Tate (ed.), 'A Personal Memoir', *T. S. Eliot: The Man and his Work* (1967)

An editor should have a pimp for a brother, so he'd have somebody to look up to.

Gene Fowler (1890–1960)

An editor is one who separates the wheat from the chaff and prints the chaff.

Adlai Stevenson (1900–65)

Bill Adler (ed.), *The Stevenson Wit* (1966)

IT WAS THE ECSTASY OF STRIKING MATCHES IN THE DARK.

Erica Jong (b. 1942)

On writing poetry

'Preface', *What Do Women Want?* (1998)

WHOM THE GODS WISH TO DESTROY THEY FIRST CALL PROMISING.

Cyril Connolly (1903–74)

Enemies of Promise (1938)

Overbearing, insensitive editors and mulish, unlistening authors, whether singly or in pairs, have caused many a shift of contract and failed book.

Alan D. Williams (1919–91)
Gerald Gross (ed.), 'What is an Editor?', *Editors on Editing* (1994)

Education

Everywhere I go I'm asked if I think the university stifles writers. My opinion is that they don't stifle enough of them. There's many a best-seller that could have been prevented by a good teacher.

Flannery O'Connor (1925–64)
Margaret Turner, 'Visit to Flannery O'Connor Proves a Novel Experience', *The Atlanta Journal and The Atlanta Constitution*, 20 May 1960

The idea that it is necessary to go to a university in order to become a successful writer, or even a man or woman of letters (which is by no means the same thing), is one of those phantasies that surround authorship.

Vera Brittain (1893–1970)
On Being an Author (1948)

The book written against fame and learning has the author's name on the title page.

Ralph Waldo Emerson (1803–82)
Journals, 1860–1866

Emotion

When those emotions are fueled into our writing, our readers have no choice but to share them [...] That, to me, is how empathy is born.

Angie Thomas (b. 1988)

'Bestseller Angie Thomas on writing, bestsellerdom, and diversity in publishing', *Nathan Bransford*, 11 December 2017

Poetry is the spontaneous overflow of powerful feelings: it takes its origin from emotion recollected in tranquillity.

William Wordsworth (1770–1850)

'Preface', *Lyrical Ballads* (1800)

No tears in the writer, no tears in the reader.

Robert Frost (1874–1963)

'The Figure a Poem Makes', *Collected Poems* (1939)

Make 'em laugh; make 'em cry; make 'em wait.

Charles Reade (1814–84)

Poetry is not a turning loose of emotion, but an escape from emotion; it is not the expression of personality, but an escape from personality.

T. S. Eliot (1888–1965)

'Tradition and the Individual Talent', *The Sacred Wood: Essays on Poetry and Criticism* (1920)

Enjoyment

Some writers enjoy writing, I am told. Not me. I enjoy
having written.
   George R. R. Martin (b. 1948)

Most people enjoy the sight of their own handwriting as
they enjoy the smell of their own farts.
   W. H. Auden (1907–73)
   'Writing', *The Dyer's Hand* (1963)

Equipment

And all writers need to make sure they have a posturally
correct chair, for the nine hundred hours a day they'll be
sitting and typing – else their lower back will compact
like plywood.
   Caitlin Moran (b. 1975)
   Eleanor Bley Griffiths, Ellie Harrison & Flora Carr, 'How to succeed as a
   screenwriter: Female writers share top tips for breaking into the TV industry',
   Radio Times, 18 October 2018

I think it is absolutely vital to have a notebook in your
hands, always, and to scribble constantly.
   William Dalrymple (b. 1965)
   Writers' & Artists' Yearbook (2006)

I do most of my work sitting down; that's where I shine.
Robert Benchley (1889–1945)
Irving Wallace, 'He Works Sitting Down', *This Week Magazine*, October 1942

[...] the good reader is one who has imagination, memory, a dictionary, and some artistic sense.
Vladimir Nabokov (1899–1977)
Lectures on Literature (1980)

Exercise

Exercising is a good analogy for writing. If you're not used to exercising you want to avoid it forever.
Jennifer Egan (b. 1962)
Meredith Maran (ed.), *In Why We Write: 20 Acclaimed Authors on How and Why They Do What They Do* (2013)

Reading is to the mind what exercise is to the body.
Joseph Addison (1672–1719)
The Tatler, 18 March 1710, no. 147

All good writing is *swimming under water* and holding your breath.
F. Scott Fitzgerald (1896–1940)
The Crack-Up: with Other Uncollected Pieces, Note-Books and Unpublished Letters (1945)

E

Fiction

The trouble with writing fiction is that it has to make sense, whereas real life doesn't.

Iain M. Banks (1954–2013)

Stuart Kelly, 'Iain Banks: The Final Interview', the *Guardian*, 15 June 2013

I do not believe that she wrote one word of fiction which does not put out boundaries a little way; one book which does not break new ground and form part of the total experiment.

Susan Hill (b. 1942)

Referring to Virginia Woolf

Daily Telegraph, 5 May 1974

Contentment and fulfilment don't make for very good fiction.

Anthony Trollope (1815–82)

Finishing

A poem is never finished; it's always an accident that puts a stop to it—that is to say, gives it to the public.

Paul Valéry (1871–1945)

Littérature (1930)

Once I have looked on it as completed [...] it becomes next to impossible to alter or amend. With the heavy suspicion on my mind that all may not be right, I yet feel forced to put up with the inevitably wrong.

Charlotte Brontë (1816–55)
Letter to her editor W.S. Williams (1849)

The artistic impulse seems not to wish to produce finished work. It certainly deserts us halfway, after the idea is born; and if we go on, art is labor.

Clarence Shepard Day (1874–1935)
This Simian World (1920)

First draft

Time enough to think and cut and rewrite tomorrow. But today-explode-fly-apart-disintegrate! The other six or seven drafts are going to be pure torture. So why not enjoy the first draft, in the hope that your joy will seek and find others in the world who, by reading your story, will catch fire, too?

Ray Bradbury (1920–2012)
Zen in the Art of Writing (1973)

Writers on Writing

On plenty of days the writer can write three or four pages, and on plenty of other days he concludes he must throw them away.

Annie Dillard (b. 1945)
The Writing Life (1989)

Get it down. Take chances. It may be bad, but it's the only way you can do anything really good.

William Faulkner (1897–1962)
A Faulkner Perspective (1976)

A first draft is the beginning of the end. But the end lasts for ever.

Matt Haig (b. 1975)
'25 rules for writing a novel', *BookTrust*

Get it all down. Let it pour out of you and onto the page. Write an incredibly shitty, self-indulgent, whiny, mewling first draft. Then take out as many of the excesses as you can.

Anne Lamott (b. 1954)
Bird by Bird: Some Instructions on Writing and Life (1994)

THE FIRST DRAFT IS JUST YOU TELLING YOURSELF THE STORY.

Terry Pratchett (1948–2015)

EVERY FIRST DRAFT IS PERFECT, BECAUSE ALL A FIRST DRAFT HAS TO DO IS EXIST.

Jane Smiley (b. 1949)

Formula

It's a formula-driven business—if you've written one book about a bricklayer, they want you to write 1,000 books about a bricklayer.

Dean Koontz (b. 1945)

Alison Beard, 'Life's Work: An Interview with Dean Koontz', *Harvard Business Review*, March–April 2020

Far too many relied on the classic formula of a beginning, a muddle, and an end.

Philip Larkin (1922–85)

New Fiction, January 1978

What is writing a novel like? The beginning: A ride through a spring wood. The middle: The Gobi desert. The end: Going down the cresta run...I am now (p. 166 of 'The Buccaneers') in the middle of the Gobi desert.

Edith Wharton (1862–1937)

Letter to Bernard Berenson, 12 January 1937
R. W. B. Lewis and Nancy Lewis (eds), *The Letters of Edith Wharton* (1988)

I'm a great believer in chaos. I don't believe that you start with a formula and then you fulfill the formula.

Sam Shepard (1943–2017)

In conversation with Clare Dwyer-Hogg, 2013

Friendship

But a writer isn't supposed to make friends with his writing, I don't think.

Joy Williams (b. 1944)
Will Blythe (ed.), *In Why I Write: Thoughts on the Craft of Fiction* (1998)

Writing is a job, a talent, but it's also the place to go in your head. It is the imaginary friend you drink your tea with in the afternoon.

Ann Patchett (b. 1963)
Truth and Beauty (2004)

A good book is the best of friends, the same today and for ever.

Martin Farquhar Tupper (1810–89)
'Of Reading', *Proverbial Philosophy: A Book of Thoughts and Arguments, Originally Treated* (1848)

A GOOD FRIEND IS A CONNECTION TO LIFE—A TIE TO THE PAST, A ROAD TO THE FUTURE, THE KEY TO SANITY IN A TOTALLY INSANE WORLD.

Lois Wyse (1926–2007)
Women Make the Best Friends: A Celebration (1995)

———————————

NO BARRIER OF THE SENSES SHUTS ME OUT FROM THE SWEET, GRACIOUS DISCOURSES OF MY BOOK FRIENDS. THEY TALK TO ME WITHOUT EMBARRASSMENT OR AWKWARDNESS.

Helen Keller (1880–1968)
The Story of My Life (1903)

———————————

G

Genius

If it is true that talent recreates life while genius has the additional gift of crowning it with myths, Melville is first and foremost a creator of myths.

Albert Camus (1913–60)

Quoted in P. Thody (ed., trans.), *Albert Camus: Selected Essays and Notebooks* (1989)

The imagination is the only genius. It is intrepid and eager and the extreme of its achievement lies in its abstraction. The achievement of the romantic, however, lies in minor wish-fulfillments and it is incapable of abstraction.

Wallace Stevens (1879–1955)

'Imagination as Value', *The Necessary Angel: Essays on Reality and the Imagination* (1951)

There are plenty of clever young writers. But there is too much genius, not enough talent.

J. B. Priestley (1894–1984)

'Sayings of the Week', *Observer*, 29 September 1968

But I fear my story fatigues you. I would like to learn. Could you tell me how to grow, or is it unconveyed, like melody or witchcraft?

Emily Dickinson (1830–86)

Letter to Thomas Wentworth Higginson

Genre

I don't think writers choose the genre, the genre chooses us. I wrote out of the wish to create order out of disorder, the liking of a pattern.

P. D. James (1920–2014)

Jake Kerridge, 'PD James, Queen of Detective Fiction: Interview', *The Telegraph*, 26 September 2009

Don't shove me into your damn pigeonhole, where I don't fit, because I'm all over. My tentacles are coming out of the pigeonhole in all directions.

Ursula K. Le Guin (1929–2018)

John Wray, 'Ursula K. Le Guin, The Art of Fiction No. 221', *The Paris Review*, Fall 2013

A Good book

All books are divisible into two classes, the books of the hour, and the books of all time.

John Ruskin (1819–1900)

'Of Kings' Treasuries', *Sesame and Lilies* (1865)

A good book is the best of friends, the same today and for ever.

Martin Farquhar Tupper (1810–89)
'Of Reading', *Proverbial Philosophy: A Book of Thoughts and Arguments, Originally Treated* (1848)

Who kills a man kills a reasonable creature, God's image; but he who destroys a good book, kills reason itself, kills the image of God, as it were in the eye.

John Milton (1608–74)
Areopagitica (1644)

I am convinced more and more day by day that fine writing is next to fine doing, the top thing in the world.

John Keats (1795–1821)
Letter to John Hamilton Reynolds, 24 August 1819
H. E. Rollins (ed.), *Letters of John Keats, Vol. 2* (1958)

Grammar

When I split an infinitive, god damn it, I split it so it stays split.

Raymond Chandler (1888–1959)
Letter to Edward Weeks, his English publisher
18 January 1947

I genuinely don't care about splitting infinitives, starting sentences with 'and' or 'but', or using 'iconic' to mean 'famous'. All of these 'sins' have been committed by writers far better than me. Pedantry is rarely the mother of creativity.

Ben Schott (b. 1974)
Writers' & Artists' Yearbook (2015)

I'm glad you like adverbs—I adore them; they are the only qualifications I really much respect.

Henry James (1843–1916)
Percy Lubbock (ed.), *The Letters of Henry James* (1920)

Writing is an act of faith, not a trick of grammar.

E. B. White (1899–1985)
'Calculating Machine', *Second Tree From the Corner* (1954)

I have that continuous uncomfortable feeling of 'things' in the head, like icebergs or rocks or awkwardly placed pieces of furniture. It's as if all the nouns were there but the verbs were lacking.

Elizabeth Bishop (1911–79)
Quoted in Robert Giroux (ed.), *One Art: The Selected Letters of Elizabeth Bishop* (1994)

Greatness

American writers want to be not good but great; and so are neither.
   Gore Vidal (1925–2012)
   Two Sisters (1970)

I would sooner fail than not be among the greatest.
   John Keats (1795–1821)
   H. E. Rollins (ed.), *Letters of John Keats* (1958)

The faults of great authors are generally excellences carried to an excess.
   Samuel Taylor Coleridge (1772–1834)
   Miscellanies (1884)

A great writer creates a world of his own and his readers are proud to live in it. A lesser writer may entice them in for a moment, but soon he will watch them filing out.
   Cyril Connolly (1903–74)
   Enemies of Promise (1938)

ƕ

Hallucinations

Dreams have always had an importance for me [...] Two novels and several short stories have emerged from my dreams, and sometimes I have had hints of what is called by the difficult name of extra-sensory perception.

Graham Greene (1904–91)
A Sort of Life (1971)

Faulkner's hallucinatory tendencies are not unworthy of Shakespeare.

Jorge Luis Borges (1899–1986)
An Introduction to American Literature (1967)

Heroes

How do we hear the woman's voice within the hero's tale? It turns out the answer is simple: make her the hero.

Madeline Miller (b. 1978)
'Witch Hunt', *Harper's Bazaar*, May 2018

Show me a hero and I will write you a tragedy.

F. Scott Fitzgerald (1896–1940)
'Notebooks E', *The Crack-Up: with Other Uncollected Pieces, Note-Books and Unpublished Letters* (1945)

The tragedy of life is that your early heroes lose their glamour...Now, with Doyle I don't have this feeling. I still revere his work as much as ever. I used to think it swell, and I still think it swell.

P. G. Wodehouse (1881–1975)
Performing Flea (1962)

A good novel tells us the truth about its hero; but a bad novel tells us the truth about its author.

G. K. Chesterton (1874–1936)
Heretics (1905)

History

A novelist is, like all mortals, more fully at home on the surface of the present than in the ooze of the past.

Vladimir Nabokov (1899–1977)
Strong Opinions (1951)

Except for Shakespeare, all writers are made to look like schoolboys by history and nature.

Georg Büchner (1813–37)
Quoted in John Reddick (trans.), *Complete Plays, Lenz and Other Writings* (1993)

Humility

Humility is not a peculiar habit of self-effacement, rather like having an inaudible voice, it is a selfless respect for reality and one of the most difficult and central of all the virtues.
Iris Murdoch (1919–99)
The Sovereignty of Good (1970)

A hefty dose of humility in writing seems to me both seemly and healthy.
Joanna Trollope (b. 1943)
Writers' & Artists' Yearbook (2006)

Humour

The comic is the perception of the opposite; humor is the feeling of it.
Umberto Eco (1932–2016)
William Weaver (trans.), *Travels in Hyperreality* (1986)

If tragedy is an experience of hyperinvolvement, comedy is an experience of underinvolvement, of detachment.
Susan Sontag (1933–2004)
Against Interpretation (1966)

I GET A LOT OF LETTERS FROM PEOPLE. THEY SAY, 'I WANT TO BE A WRITER. WHAT SHOULD I DO?' I TELL THEM TO STOP WRITING TO ME AND GET ON WITH IT.

Ruth Rendell (1930–2015)

Humor is emotional chaos remembered in tranquility.

James Thurber (1894–1961)

New York Post, 29 February 1960

Humour is the first of the gifts to perish in a foreign tongue.

Virginia Woolf (1882–1941)

The Common Reader: Volume 1 (2003)

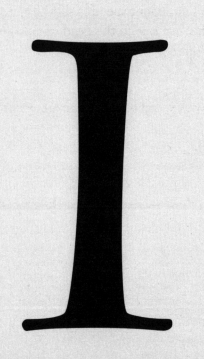

Ideas

I shouldn't complain, but really, I have too many ideas. They line up like urgent spectres shouting 'me, me!' until I give in and beckon one to the head of the queue.

Emma Donoghue (b. 1969)
'An Exclusive Interview with Emma Donoghue', *SheWrites*, 24 September 2019

Do change your mind. Good ideas are often murdered by better ones.

Roddy Doyle (b. 1958)
'Ten rules for writing fiction', the *Guardian*, 20 February 2010

Novels, even short stories, eat ideas like forest fires eat trees.

Patrick Ness (b. 1971)
'Patrick Ness' guide to writing: Getting started', *BookTrust*

Dying for an idea, again, sounds well enough, but why not let the idea die instead of you?

Wyndham Lewis (1882–1957)
The Art of Being Ruled (1926)

I

Idleness

I don't think necessity is the mother of invention—invention, in my opinion, arises directly from idleness, possibly also from laziness. To save oneself trouble.
Agatha Christie (1890–1976)
An Autobiography (1977)

When I am in the country I wish to vegetate like the country.
William Hazlitt (1778–1830)
'On Going a Journey', *Table Talk* (1821)

It is impossible to enjoy idling thoroughly unless one has plenty of work to do.
Jerome K. Jerome (1859–1927)
Idle Thoughts of an Idle Fellow (1886)

Ignorance

People say to write about what you know. I'm here to tell you, no one wants to read that, cos you don't know anything. So write about something you don't know. And don't be scared, ever.
Toni Morrison (1931–2019)
Rebecca Sutton, 'Write, Erase, Do It Over', *American Artscape*, Issue 4 (2014)

What you don't know would make a great book.

Sydney Smith (1771–1845)

Lady Holland, *A Memoir of the Rev. Sydney Smith* (1855)

Ignorance, arrogance, and racism have bloomed as Superior Knowledge in all too many universities.

Alice Walker (b. 1944)

The Alice Walker Collection Non-Fiction (2013)

Until you understand a writer's ignorance, presume yourself ignorant of his understanding.

Samuel Taylor Coleridge (1772–1834)

Biographia Literaria (1817)

Imaginary worlds

I am interested in how hard it has been, historically, for humans to figure out their place in the world and how to thrive in it. One of the techniques that they use to cope is to imagine a world outside of the one they occupy and to invest that world with all sorts of powerful beings.

Deborah Harkness (b. 1965)

Laure-Blaise McDowell, 'Exclusive Interview with "A Discovery of Witches" Author Deborah Harkness', *Bookstr*, 24 May 2019

I

I write about imaginary countries, alien societies on other planets, dragons, wizards, the Napa Valley in 2002. I know these things. I know them better than anybody else possibly could, so it's my duty to testify about them.

Ursula K. Le Guin (1929–2018)

John Wray, 'Ursula K. Le Guin, The Art of Fiction No. 221', *The Paris Review*, Fall 2013

There are many reasons why novelists write, but they all have one thing in common—a need to create an alternative world.

John Fowles (1926–2005)

Sunday Times Magazine, 2 October 1977

Imagination

If one is lucky, a solitary fantasy can totally transform one million realities.

Maya Angelou (1928–2014)

The Heart of a Woman (1981)

To treat your facts with imagination is one thing, to imagine your facts is another.

John Burroughs (1837–1921)

Clara Barrus (ed.), *The Heart of Burroughs Journals* (1967)

Imagination doesn't fall from the sky; you have to work with something.

Chimamanda Ngozi Adichie (b. 1977)

Aaron Bady, 'Chimamanda Ngozi Adichie: "Race doesn't occur to me"', *Boston Review*, 14 July 2013

Imagination is not an empirical or superadded power of consciousness, it is the whole of consciousness as it realizes its freedom.

Jean-Paul Sartre (1905–80)

The Psychology of Imagination (1948)

Imagination...is the irrepressible revolutionist.

Wallace Stevens (1879–1955)

'Imagination as Value', *The Necessary Angel: Essays on Reality and the Imagination* (1951)

In countries where the imagination of the people, and the language they use, is rich and living, it is possible for a writer to be rich and copious in his words, and at the same time to give the reality, which is the root of all poetry, in a comprehensive and natural form.

J. M. Synge (1871–1909)

'Preface', *The Playboy of the Western World* (1907)

Imagination and fiction make up more than three quarters of our real life.

Simone Weil (1909–43)

Gravity and Grace (2002)

The poet...will decide to do as the imagination bids, because he has no choice, if he is to remain a poet. Poetry is the imagination of life.

Wallace Stevens (1879–1955)

'The Figure of the Youth as Virile Poet', *The Necessary Angel: Essays on Reality and the Imagination* (1951)

Insanity

There are every year works published whose contents show them to be by real lunatics.

William James (1842–1910)

The Principles of Psychology, Vol. 1 (1890)

Everyone is always warning you not to do something as mad as to try and write a novel.

Isabella Hammad (b. 1992)

Alessandra Codinha, 'Sentimental Education', *Vogue*, April 2019

Pound's crazy. All poets are...They have to be. You don't put a poet like Pound in the loony bin. For history's sake we shouldn't keep him there.

Ernest Hemingway (1899–1961)

Quoted in Leonard Lyons, *New York Post* (1957)

I MUST HAVE A PRODIGIOUS
QUANTITY OF MIND; IT TAKES
ME AS MUCH AS A WEEK,
SOMETIMES, TO MAKE IT UP.

Mark Twain (1835–1910)
The Innocents Abroad (1869)

———————

YOUR INTUITION KNOWS
WHAT TO WRITE, SO GET
OUT OF THE WAY.

Ray Bradbury (1920–2012)

———————

I

Why do some poets manage to get by and live to be malicious old bores like Frost or—probably—pompous old ones like Yeats, or crazy old ones like Pound—and some just don't!

Elizabeth Bishop (1911–79)
Quoted in Robert Giroux (ed.), *One Art: The Selected Letters of Elizabeth Bishop* (1994)

Kipling tries so hard to celebrate and justify true authority, the work and habit and wisdom of the world, because he feels so bitterly the abyss of pain and insanity that they overlie.

Randall Jarrell (1914–65)
'On Preparing to Read Kipling', *Kipling, Auden, & Co.: Essays and Reviews, 1935–1964* (1981)

Writers come in two principal categories—those who are overtly insecure and those who are covertly insecure—and they can all use help.

John McPhee (b. 1931)
Draft No. 4 (2017)

Inspiration

You often come across the best stories when you least expect them.
William Dalrymple (b. 1965)
Writers' & Artists' Yearbook (2006)

And, nearing the age of 40, I'd already used up many of the usual tricks writers before me had employed to shake things up when they were in a rut: travel chemically, break your heart, change continents, get married, have a child, quit your job, etc.
Mohsin Hamid (b. 1971)
Joe Fassler, 'Get Fit With Haruki Murakami: Why Mohsin Hamid Exercises, Then Writes', *The Atlantic*, 5 March 2013

You can't wait for inspiration. You have to go after it with a club.
Jack London (1876–1916)
Jack London on Adventure: Words of Wisdom from an Expert Adventurer (2015)

I cannot summon up inspiration; I myself am summoned.
P. L. Travers (1899–1996)
Edwina Burness & Jerry Griswold, 'P. L. Travers, The Art of Fiction No. 63', *The Paris Review*, Winter 1982

Intellect

Shaw's judgements are often scatterbrained, but at least he has brains to scatter.

Max Beerbohm (1872–1956)

S. N. Behrman, *Conversations with Max* (1960)

At 83 Shaw's mind was perhaps not quite as good as it used to be, but it was still better than anyone else's.

Alexander Woollcott (1887–1943)

While Rome Burns (1934)

Drama is the back-stairs of the intellect. Philosophers and historians go in by the front door, but playwrights and novelists sneak up the back stairs with their more disreputable luggage.

Alan Bennett (b. 1934)

Sunday Times, 24 November 1991

My work as a writer has from the beginning aimed at tracing the lightning flashes of the mental circuits that capture and link points distant from each other in time and space.

Italo Calvino (1923–85)

'Quickness', *Six Memos for the Next Millennium* (1988)

Clever men are good, but they are not the best.
Thomas Carlyle (1795–1881)
'Goethe', *Edinburgh Review*, 1828

I love to lose myself in other men's minds. When I am not walking, I am reading; I cannot sit and think. Books think for me.
Charles Lamb (1775–1834)
'Detached Thoughts on Books and Reading', *Last Essays of Elia* (1833)

Isolation

Good novels are produced by people who voluntarily isolate themselves, and go deep, and report from the depths on what they find.
Jonathan Franzen (b. 1959)
Joe Fassler, 'Marcus Aurelius's One Question to Beat Procrastination, Whining, and Struggle', *The Atlantic*, 28 May 2013

I really advise against becoming a hermit.
Adele Parks (b. 1969)
Writers' & Artists' Yearbook (2011)

J

K

Journalism

Journalism largely consists in saying 'Lord Jones is dead'
to people who never knew Lord Jones was alive.
G. K. Chesterton (1874–1936)

Journalism is the only job that requires no degrees, no
diplomas and no specialised knowledge of any kind.
Patrick Campbell (1913–80)
My Life and Easy Times (1967)

Literature is the art of writing something that will be read
twice; journalism what will be grasped at once.
Cyril Connolly (1903–74)
Enemies of Promise (1938)

The life of the journalist is poor, nasty, brutish and short.
So is his style.
Stella Gibbons (1902–89)
'Foreword', *Cold Comfort Farm* (1932)

It rots a writer's brain, it cretinizes you. You say the same
thing again and again, and when you do that happily
you're well on the way to being a cretin. Or a politician.
John Updike (1932–2009)
'Interview', *Observer*, 30 August 1987

I act as a sponge. I soak it up and squeeze it out in ink every two weeks.

Janet Flanner (1892–1978)
Irving Drutman (ed.), *Paris Was Yesterday, 1925–1939* (1972)

Judgement

Put down everything that comes into your head and then you're a writer. But an author is one who can judge his own stuff's worth, without pity, and destroy most of it.

Colette (1873–1954)

I went for years not finishing anything because, of course, when you finish something you can be judged.

Erica Jong (b. 1942)
Fear of Flying (1973)

Just write

One of the few things I know about writing is this: spend it all, shoot it, play it, lose it, all, right away, every time. Do not hoard what seems good for a later place in the book, or for another book; give it, give it all, give it now.

Annie Dillard (b. 1945)
The Writing Life (1989)

Nothing will work unless you do.
Maya Angelou (1928–2014)
'Maya Angelou quotes: 15 of the best', the *Guardian*, 29 May 2014

No amount of self-inflicted misery, altered states, black pullovers or being publicly obnoxious will ever add up to your being a writer. Writers write. On you go.
A. L. Kennedy (b. 1965)
'Ten rules for writing fiction', the *Guardian*, 20 February 2010

Looking back, I imagine I was always writing. Twaddle it was too. But better far write twaddle or anything, anything, than nothing at all.
Katherine Mansfield (1888–1923)
John Middleton Murry (ed.), *Journal of Katherine Mansfield* (1927)

Keep going

Being a writer is tantamount to becoming a writer, and that process of becoming—reading, thinking, observing, learning, struggling, discovering, doubting, writing, erasing and rewriting—is an open-ended journey. You never arrive anywhere, really. You just keep going.
Elif Shafak (b. 1971)
'Elif Shafak on Becoming a Writer', *Waterstones Blog*, 28 August 2020

THREE THINGS IN HUMAN LIFE ARE IMPORTANT. THE FIRST IS TO BE KIND. THE SECOND IS TO BE KIND. AND THE THIRD IS TO BE KIND.

Henry James (1843–1916)

Quoted in Leon Edel, *Henry James: A Life* (1953)

———————————

I put the words down and push them a bit.
Evelyn Waugh (1903–66)
Quoted in Obituary, *New York Times*

And so when it's difficult, what keeps me going is the possibility of joy.
Chimamanda Ngozi Adichie (b. 1977)

Abandon the idea that you are ever going to finish. Lose track of the 400 pages and write just one page for each day; it helps.
John Steinbeck (1902–68)
George Plimpton & Frank Crowther, 'John Steinbeck, The Art of Fiction No. 45 (Continued)', *The Paris Review*, Fall 1975

If you write one story, it may be bad; if you write a hundred, you have the odds in your favor.
Edgar Rice Burroughs (1875–1950)
John Miller, 'King of the Jungle', *reason*, August/September 1999

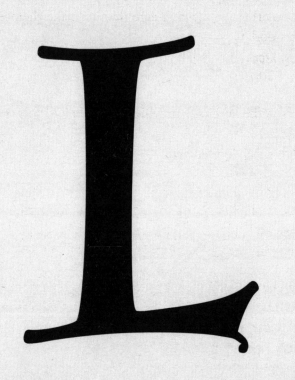

Language

The most incomprehensible talk comes from people who have no other use for language than to make themselves understood.

Karl Kraus (1874–1936)
Harry Zohn (ed.), *In These Great Times: A Karl Kraus Reader* (1976)

Poetry is the language in which man explores his own amazement.

Christopher Fry (1907–2005)
Time, 3 April 1950

For poets, language is a maze, not a way forward.

Song Lin (b. 1959)
'Prison Letter', *Under-Sky Underground: Chinese Writing Today* (1994)

Language imparts identity, meaning, and perspective to our human condition. Writers are either polluters or part of the cleanup.

Mary Pipher (b. 1947)
Writing to Change the World (2007)

L

Understanding words does not consist in knowing their dictionary definitions...Understanding language is more like understanding cricket: it is a matter of habits, acquired in oneself and rightly presumed in others.

Bertrand Russell (1872–1970)
The Analysis of Mind (1921)

Language can only deal meaningfully with a special, restricted segment of reality. The rest, and it is presumably the much larger part, is silence.

George Steiner (1929–2020)
'The Retreat from the Word', *Language and Silence* (Macmillan 1967)

Language grows out of life, out of its needs and experiences.

Anne Sullivan (1866–1936)
Speech to the American Association to Promote the Teaching of Speech to the Deaf, July 1894

We die. That may be the meaning of life. But we do language. That may be the measure of our lives.

Toni Morrison (1931–2019)
'Nobel Lecture', The Nobel Prize, 7 December 1993

I HAVE TRIED TO REMOVE WEIGHT, SOMETIMES FROM PEOPLE, SOMETIMES FROM HEAVENLY BODIES, SOMETIMES FROM CITIES; ABOVE ALL I HAVE TRIED TO REMOVE WEIGHT FROM THE STRUCTURE OF STORIES AND FROM LANGUAGE.

Italo Calvino (1923–85)
Six Memos for the Next Millennium (1988)

———————————

LANGUAGE IS THE ROAD MAP OF A CULTURE. IT TELLS YOU WHERE ITS PEOPLE COME FROM AND WHERE THEY ARE GOING.

Rita Mae Brown (b. 1944)
Starting from Scratch (1988)

———————————

L

Laziness

I make no secret of the fact that I would rather lie on a sofa than sweep beneath it. But you have to be efficient if you're going to be lazy.

> **Shirley Conran** (b. 1932)
> *Superwoman* (1975)

The more important virtue for a writer, I believe, is self-forgiveness. Because your writing will always disappoint you. Your laziness will always disappoint you.

> **Elizabeth Gilbert** (b. 1969)
> 'Thoughts on Writing', www.elizabethgilbert.com/thoughts-on-writing/

If one is too lazy to think, too vain to do a thing badly, too cowardly to admit it, one will never attain wisdom.

> **Cyril Connolly** (1903–74)
> Written under the pseudonym Palinurus
> *The Unquiet Grave* (1944)

Libraries

The very existence of libraries affords the best evidence that we may yet have hope for the future of man.

> **T. S. Eliot** (1888–1965)

**FROM THE MOMENT
I PICKED UP YOUR BOOK
UNTIL I LAID IT DOWN,
I WAS CONVULSED WITH
LAUGHTER. SOME DAY
I INTEND READING IT.**

Groucho Marx (1890–1977)

S. J. Perelman, *The Last Laugh* (2000)

———————————

L

[Libraries are] safe, warm, free places where anyone can learn to read, to dream, to use English, sometimes, or a computer – or, perhaps, to be a writer.

Maggie Gee (b. 1948)
Writers' & Artists' Yearbook (2012)

When a man writes from his own mind, he writes very rapidly. The greatest part of a writer's time is spent in reading, in order to write; a man will turn over half a library to make one book.

Samuel Johnson (1709–84)
James Boswell, *Life of Samuel Johnson* (1992)

A library is thought in cold storage.

Herbert Samuel (1870–1963)
A Book of Quotations (1947)

Lies

It is important to remember that lies (white or whoppers) and luck (of both kinds) may play a disproportionately large part in the way things turn out.

Mark Billingham (b. 1961)
Writers' & Artists' Yearbook (2006)

Lying is the beginning of fiction.
Jamaica Kincaid (b. 1949)
New York Times, 7 October 1990

The cruellest lies are often told in silence.
Robert Louis Stevenson (1850–94)
Virginibus Puerisque (1881)

The lies of novels are never gratuitous: they compensate for the inadequacies of life.
Mario Vargas Llosa (b. 1936)
The Truth of Lies (1989)

The thing that makes poetry different from all of the other arts...is you're using language, which is what you use for everything else—telling lies and selling socks, advertising, and conducting law. Whereas we don't write little concerts or paint little pictures.
W. S. Merwin (1927–2019)
Said on receiving the inaugural $100,000 Tanning Prize for poetry (now the Wallace Stevens Award) in 1995
Quoted in *Washington Post*

L

Life

Imagine thinking that black people write only about being black and not about being people.

Alice Walker (b. 1944)

'Fame', *You Can't Keep a Good Woman Down* (1981)

Books are good enough in their own way, but they are a mighty bloodless substitute for life.

Robert Louis Stevenson (1850–94)

Virginibus Puerisque (1881)

Writers can't back off from realism, just as an ambitious engineer cannot back off from electricity.

Tom Wolfe (1930–2018)

Heath Hardage, '"Never Try To Fit In" Tom Wolfe Advises Young Writers', *The Richmond News Leader*, 3 November 1987

Too many people in the modern world view poetry as a luxury, not a necessity like petrol. But to me it's the oil of life.

John Betjeman (1906–84)

'Sayings of the Year', *Observer*, 1974

It does not matter that Dickens' world is not life-like; it is alive.

David Cecil (1902–86)

Early Victorian Novelists (1934)

Lifeblood

To search the heart is poetry's lifeblood.
Cai Qijiao (1918–2007)
Quoted in Edward Morin (ed.), *The Red Azalea* (1991)

If I read a book and it makes my whole body so cold no
fire can ever warm me, I know that is poetry. If I feel
physically as if the top of my head were taken off, I know
that is poetry. These are the only ways I know it. Is there
any other way?
Emily Dickinson (1830–86)
Selected Letters (1986)

A good book is the precious life-blood of a master spirit,
embalmed and treasured up on purpose to a life beyond
life.
John Milton (1608–74)
Areopagitica (1644)

Loss

People always are encouraging about a terrible loss, so that
sometimes the loser would like to strangle them.
Garrison Keillor (b. 1942)
'Preface', *Lake Wobegon Days* (1985)

I think that if a third of all the novelists and maybe two-thirds of all the poets now writing dropped dead suddenly, the loss to literature would not be great.

Charles Osbourne (1927–2017)

Remark made in 1985

Love and lust

It's much easier to write about young love and young lust than it is about middle-aged lust. I mean, who cares?

André Aciman (b. 1951)

Jessica Gross, 'An Interview with "Call Me By Your Name" Author André Aciman', *Longreads*, November 2017

To write is an act of love. If it isn't it's just writing.

Jean Cocteau (1889–1963)

'Des Moeurs', *La Difficulté d'être* (1947)

When one is in love, one writes very well.

Elena Ferrante (b. 1943)

Didier Jacob, 'In a rare interview, Elena Ferrante describes the writing process behind the Neapolitan novels', *Los Angeles Times*, 17 May 2018

Marry somebody you love and who thinks you being a writer's a good idea.

Richard Ford (b. 1944)

'Ten rules for writing fiction', the *Guardian*, 20 February 2010

You can, of course, steal stories and attributes from family and friends, fill in filecards after lovemaking and so forth. It might be better to celebrate those you love—and love itself—by writing in such a way that everyone keeps their privacy and dignity intact.

A. L. Kennedy (b. 1965)
Phil Daoust (ed.), *Write* (2012)

Luck

Luck in fiction is very much a lottery, and it depends at the present time not so much on what you say as how you say it.

G. E. Mitton (1868–1955)
Writers' & Artists' Yearbook (1933)

Writing is like getting married. One should never commit oneself until one is amazed at one's luck.

Iris Murdoch (1919–99)
The Black Prince (1973)

Madness

Perhaps no person can be a poet, or can even enjoy poetry, without a certain unsoundness of mind.

Thomas Babington Macaulay (1800–59)
'On Milton', *Essays Contributed to the Edinburgh Review* (1843)

The courage of the poet is to keep ajar the door that leads to madness.

Christopher Darlington Morley (1890–1957)
Inward Ho! (1923)

All poets are mad.

Robert Burton (1577–1640)
'Democritus to the Reader', *The Anatomy of Melancholy* (1621)

One always writes comedy at the moment of deepest hysteria.

V. S. Naipaul (1932–2018)
'Sayings of the Week', *Observer*, 1 May 1994

Marriage

Poetry was the maiden I loved, but politics was the harridan I married.

Joseph Howe (1804–73)

Poets should never marry. The world should thank me for not marrying you.
   Maud Gonne (1866–1953)

The Media

The only thing I don't like about the press is I can give as many answers as you want, and be totally honest, but finally it's you who shapes the final product...often what comes out isn't what I meant at all.
   Roddy Doyle (b. 1958)
   Observer, 1 May 1994

Media is a word that has come to mean bad journalism.
   Graham Greene (1904–91)
   Ways of Escape (1981)

Comment is free but facts are sacred.
   C. P. Scott (1846–1932)
   'A Hundred Years', *Manchester Guardian*, 5 May 1921

Journalism could be described as turning one's enemies into money.
   Craig Brown (b. 1957)
   Daily Telegraph, 28 September 1990

Medicine

To read the poems of Pasternak is to get one's throat clear, to fortify one's breathing, to renovate one's lungs; such poems must be a cure for tuberculosis. At present we have no poetry healthier than this. This is *kumys* after tinned milk.

Osip Mandelstam (1891–1938)
Quoted in Donald Davie & Angela Livingstone (eds), *Pasternak* (1970)

A well chosen anthology is a complete dispensary of medicine for the more common mental disorders, and may be used as much for prevention as cure.

Robert Graves (1895–1985)
On English Poetry (1922)

I suffer from the disease of writing and being ashamed of them when they are finished.

Montesquieu (1689–1755)
Pensées et fragments inédits (1899)

Metaphor

Deprivation is for me what daffodils were for Wordsworth.

Philip Larkin (1922–85)
Required Writing (1983)

Cut out the metaphors and similes. In my first book I promised myself I wouldn't use any and I slipped up during a sunset in chapter 11. I still blush when I come across it.

Esther Freud (b. 1963)
'Ten rules for writing fiction', the *Guardian*, 20 February 2010

The metaphor is probably the most fertile power possessed by man.

José Ortega y Gasset (1883–1955)
The Dehumanization of Art and Other Essays on Art, Culture, and Literature (1968)

Mightier than the sword

From this it is clear how much more cruel the pen is than the sword.

Robert Burton (1577–1640)
The Anatomy of Melancholy (1621)

We all know that books burn—yet we have the greater knowledge that books cannot be killed by fire. People die, but books never die. No man and no force can abolish memory...In this war, we know, books are weapons.

Franklin D. Roosevelt (1882–1945)
Message to the American Booksellers Association, 6 May 1942

If a line of poetry strays into my memory, my skin bristles so that the razor ceases to act.

A. E. Housman (1859–1936)

Leslie Stephen Lecture, University of Cambridge, 9 May 1933

Misquotations

Misquotations are the only quotations that are never misquoted.

Hesketh Pearson (1887–1964)

'Introduction', *Common Misquotations* (1934)

A widely-read man never quotes accurately...
Misquotation is the pride and privilege of the learned.

Hesketh Pearson (1887–1964)

'Introduction', *Common Misquotations* (1934)

Famous remarks are seldom quoted correctly.

Simeon Strunsky (1879–1948)

No Mean City (1944)

Money

Right now, forget about money. It eats imagination.

Matt Haig (b. 1975)

'25 rules for writing a novel', *BookTrust*

Fiction that isn't an author's personal adventure into the frightening or the unknown isn't worth writing for anything but money.

Jonathan Franzen (b. 1959)

'Ten rules for writing fiction', the *Guardian*, 20 February 2010

No man but a blockhead ever wrote, except for money.

Samuel Johnson (1709–84)

James Boswell, *Life of Samuel Johnson* (1791)

I loathe writing. On the other hand, I'm a great believer in money.

S. J. Perelman (1904–79)

Interview, *Life*, 1962

Are you serious about this? Then get an accountant.

Hilary Mantel (b. 1952)

'Ten rules for writing fiction', the *Guardian*, 20 February 2010

The ones I like…are 'cheque' and 'enclosed'.

Dorothy Parker (1893–1967)

On the most beautiful words in the English language
Quoted in *The New York Herald Tribune*, 12 December 1932

Motive

Oh, to have a motive! What a beautiful idea. The next time I write a book, I'm going to try that.

Emma Straub (b. 1980)

Greg Mania, 'Adulting in Motion: The Millions Interviews Emma Straub', *The Millions*, 1 May 2020

There are two motives for reading a book: one, that you enjoy it, the other that you can boast about it.

Bertrand Russell (1872–1970)

The Conquest of Happiness (1930)

All writers are vain, selfish and lazy, and at the very bottom of their motives lies a mystery.

George Orwell (1903–50)

'Why I Write', *Gangrel*, No. 4, Summer 1946

My motive is to expose the illness in order to induce people to pay attention to its cure.

Lu Xun (1881–1936)

'How I Came to Write Fiction', *Literature of the People's Republic of China* (1980)

Murder

One is fascinated by the problem of finding a method of murder that is quite right, both for the perpetrator and the victim. That is a technical problem I enjoy. So sometimes the murder is violent because I know the murderer would be violent.

P. D. James (1920–2014)

Jake Kerridge, 'PD James, Queen of Detective Fiction: Interview', *The Telegraph*, 26 September 2009

My brother-in-law wrote an unusual murder story. The victim got killed by a man from another book.

Robert Sylvester (1907–75)

For every [...] novel with a protagonist of colour, there are about 10 books about gruff white cops falling in love with murdered white women, 10 'girl' books about murderous white women, and 10 more about serial killers in Scandinavia.

Steph Cha (b. 1986)

David Barnett, 'Unusual suspects: the writers diversifying detective fiction', the *Guardian*, 15 June 2018

When in doubt have a man come through a door with a gun in his hand.

Raymond Chandler (1888–1959)

'The Simple Art of Murder', *Saturday Review of Literature*, April 1950

Muse

No one learns much by sitting at a desk waiting for 'the Muse' to knock on the door.

Adele Parks (b. 1969)

Writers' & Artists' Yearbook (2011)

I don't go up against my writing and come out bloody-knuckled. I don't wrestle with the muse. I don't argue. I try to remain stubborn in my gladness.

Elizabeth Gilbert (b. 1969)

Joe Fassler, 'The "Stubborn Gladness" of Elizabeth Gilbert's Favorite Poet', *The Atlantic*, 6 November 2013

Perversity is the muse of modern literature.

Susan Sontag (1933–2004)

Against Interpretation (1966)

Music

Poetry is a comforting piece of fiction set to more or less lascivious music.

H. L. Mencken (1880–1956)

'The Poet and his Art', *Prejudices: Third Series* (1922)

Music begins to atrophy when it departs too far from the dance;...poetry begins to atrophy when it gets too far from music.

Ezra Pound (1885–1972)

'Warning', *ABC of Reading* (1934)

Having verse set to music is like looking at a painting through a stained glass window.

Paul Valéry (1871–1945)

Metric derives from the dance; the music of poetry is therefore addressed to and originates in the muscles...Like music and painting, it arises from the total organism.

Guy Davenport (1927–2005)

The Geography of the Imagination (1981)

DEVELOP AN INTEREST IN LIFE AS YOU SEE IT; THE PEOPLE, THINGS LITERATURE. MUSIC—THE WORLD IS SO RICH, SIMPLY THROBBING, WITH RICH TREASURES, BEAUTIFUL SOULS AND INTERESTING PEOPLE. FORGET YOURSELF.

Henry Miller (1891–1980)

n

Narcissism

A narcissist is someone better looking than you are.
Gore Vidal (1925–2012)
San Francisco Chronicle, 12 April 1981

You have to be narcissistic to be an artist. You have to think you are the centre of the whole thing otherwise why do you create?
Marjane Satrapi (b. 1969)
Simon Hattenstone, 'Confessions of Miss Mischief', the *Guardian*, 29 March 2008

A good stylist should have a narcissistic enjoyment as he works. He must be able to objectivize his work to such an extent that he catches himself feeling envious...In short, he must display that highest degree of objectivity which the world calls vanity.
Karl Kraus (1874–1936)
Harry Zohn (ed.), *Half-Truths and One-And-A-Half-Truths: Selected Aphorisms* (1976)

Night

You never have to change anything you got up in the middle of the night to write.
Saul Bellow (1915–2005)

n

At night, when the objective world has slunk back into its caverns and left dreamers to their own, there come inspirations and capabilities impossible at any less magical and quiet hour. No one knows whether or not he is a writer unless he has tried writing at night.

H. P. Lovecraft (1890–1937)

Decide when in the day (or night) it best suits you to write, and organise your life accordingly.

Andrew Motion (b. 1952)

'Ten rules for writing fiction (Part two)', the *Guardian*, 20 February 2010

Has anybody ever seen a dramatic critic in the daytime? Of course not. They come out after dark, up to no good.

P. G. Wodehouse (1881–1975)

Non-fiction

Writing nonfiction is more like sculpture, a matter of shaping the research into the finished thing.

Joan Didion (b. 1934)

Hilton Als, 'Joan Didion, The Art of Nonfiction No. 1', *The Paris Review*, Spring 2006

There is no longer any such thing as fiction or non-fiction; there's only narrative.

E. L. Doctorow (1931–2015)
Quoted in *New York Times* Book Review

Novels

When I want to read a novel I write one.
Benjamin Disraeli (1804–81)
W. Monypenny & G. Buckle, *Life of Benjamin Disraeli* (1929)

Certainly one knows more at forty than one did at twenty. And contrary to all American mythology, the novel is the rightful province not of the young but of the middle-aged.
Gore Vidal (1925–2012)
'On Revising One's Own Work', *New York Times* Book Review, 14 November 1965

The story is a piece of work. The novel is a way of life.
Toni Cade Bambara (1939–1995)
J. Sternberg (ed.), 'What It Is I Think I'm Doing Anyhow', *The Writer on Her Work* (1980)

Yes—oh dear, yes—the novel tells a story.
E. M. Forster (1879–1970)
Aspects of the Novel (1927)

I WROTE MY FIRST NOVEL BECAUSE I WANTED TO READ IT.

Toni Morrison (1931–2019)

Quoted in Charles Ruas, *Conversations with American Writers* (1994)

———————————

THE DETECTIVE NOVEL IS THE ART-FOR-ART'S-SAKE OF YAWNING PHILISTINISM.

V. S. Pritchett (1900–97)

'Books in General', *New Statesman*, 16 June 1951

———————————

n

A novel is a daily labour over a period of years. A story can be like a mad, lovely visitor, with whom you spend a rather exciting weekend.

Lorrie Moore (b. 1957)

Elizabeth Gaffney, 'Lorrie Moore, The Art of Fiction No. 167', *The Paris Review*, Spring-Summer 2001

Writing a novel is a terrible experience, during which the hair often falls out and the teeth decay. I'm always irritated by people who imply that writing fiction is an escape from reality. It is a plunge into reality and it's very shocking to the system.

Flannery O'Connor (1925–64)

Mystery and Manners: Occasional Prose (1969)

A novelist can do anything he wants so long as he makes people believe in it.

Gabriel García Márquez (1927–2014)

Peter Stone, 'Gabriel García Márquez, The Art of Fiction No. 69', *The Paris Review*, Winter 1981

Writing a novel is actually searching for victims. As I write I keep looking for casualties.

John Irving (b. 1942)

Ron Hansen, 'John Irving, The Art of Fiction No. 93', *The Paris Review*, Summer-Fall 1986

Obituaries

There's no such thing as bad publicity except your own obituary.

Brendan Behan (1923–64)

Dominic Behan, *My Brother Brendan* (1965)

I've just read that I am dead. Don't forget to delete me from your list of subscribers.

Rudyard Kipling (1865–1936)

The report of my death was an exaggeration.

Mark Twain (1835–1910)

New York Journal, 2 June 1897

When I am dead, I hope it may be said:
'His sins were scarlet, but his books were read.'

Hilaire Belloc (1870–1953)

The Augustan Books of Modern Poetry: Hilaire Belloc (1925)

Originality

Be regular and orderly in your life, so that you may be violent and original in your work.

Gustave Flaubert (1821–80)

Quoted in Ira Nadal, 'Preface', *Philip Roth: A Counter Life* (1986)

O

A thought is often original, though you have uttered it a hundred times. It has come to you over a new route, by a new and express train of associations.
Oliver Wendell Holmes (1841–1935)
The Autocrat of the Breakfast-Table (1858)

All good things which exist are the fruits of originality.
John Stuart Mill (1806–73)
On Liberty (1859)

Thank goodness I was never sent to school; it would have rubbed off some of the originality.
Beatrix Potter (1866–1943)
Quoted in Anne Stevenson Hobbs, *Beatrix Potter: Artists & Illustrator* (2005)

The notion of doing something impossibly new usually turns out to be an illusion.
Twyla Tharp (b. 1941)
Independent, 8 December 1995

Everything of importance has been said before by somebody who did not discover it.
A. N. Whitehead (1861–1947)
Quoted in J. R. Newman, *The World of Mathematics* (1956)

What matters is how you bake the cake: every decent author should have their own recipe and the best find new things to add to the mix.

Terry Pratchett (1948–2015)

Writers' & Artists' Yearbook (2006)

One reason for writing, of course, is that no-one's written what you want to read.

Philip Larkin (1922–85)

Robert Phillips, 'The Art of Poetry No. 30', *The Paris Review*, Summer 1982

P

Passion

If you do not breathe through writing, if you do not
cry out in writing, or sing in writing, then don't write,
because our culture has no use for it.

Anaïs Nin (1903–77)

'The New Woman', *In Favour of the Sensitive Man and Other Essays* (1976)

Write what you feel strongly about, in the way that most
attracts you. It should be bold, personal, entertaining,
challenging and stimulating.

Lee Hall (b. 1966)

Writers' & Artists' Yearbook (1998)

Few writers have shown a more extraordinary compass of
powers than Donne; for he combined what no other man
has ever done—the last sublimation of subtlety with the
most impassioned majesty.

Thomas De Quincey (1785–1859)

Blackwood's Magazine, December 1828

No passion in the world is equal to the passion to alter
someone else's draft.

H. G. Wells (1866–1946)

George Plimpton (ed.), *The Writer's Chapbook* (1989)

Pens and pencils

I like the feeling of fountain pen. I like uncapping it. I like the weight of it in my hand.

Neil Gaiman (b. 1960)

Tim Ferris, 'The Tim Feriss Show Transcripts: Neil Gaiman', *The Tim Ferris Show* Blog, 30 March 2019

No man was more foolish when he had not a pen in his hand, or more wise when he had.

Samuel Johnson (1709–84)

James Boswell, *Life of Samuel Johnson* (1992)

The way to write a book is to actually write a book. A pen is useful, typing is also good. Keep putting words on the page.

Anne Enright (b. 1962)

'Ten rules for writing fiction', the *Guardian*, 20 February 2010

Take a pencil to write with on aeroplanes. Pens leak. But if the pencil breaks, you can't sharpen it on the plane, because you can't take knives with you. Therefore: take two pencils.

Margaret Atwood (b. 1939)

'Ten rules for writing fiction', the *Guardian*, 20 February 2010

Stevenson seemed to pick the right word up on the point of his pen, like a man playing spillikins.

G. K. Chesterton (1874–1936)
The Victorian Age in Literature (1913)

Perfection

People say that perfectionism is bad. But it's because of perfectionists that man walked on the moon and painted the Sistine Chapel, OK? Perfectionism is good.

Donna Tartt (b. 1963)
Katherine Viner, 'A talent to tantalise', the *Guardian*, 19 October 2002

Far rather would I never publish more, than publish anything inferior to my first effort.

Charlotte Brontë (1816–55)
Letter to W.S. Williams, 4 February 1849

Perspective

One gains a double benefit in writing about the past, conjuring up how things might have been, and at the same time acquiring a different perspective on the present.

Robert Harris (b. 1957)

Try to read your own work as a stranger would read it, or even better, as an enemy would.

Zadie Smith (b. 1975)

'Ten rules for writing fiction (Part two)', the *Guardian*, 20 February 2010

[I am] not an optimist but a meliorist.

George Eliot (1819–80)

Archie Burnett, *The Letters of A. E. Housman* (2007)

It's useful to go out of this world and see it from the perspective of another one.

Terry Pratchett (1948–2015)

The task I set myself technically in writing a book from eighteen different points of view and in as many styles, [...] would be enough to upset anyone's mental balance.

James Joyce (1882–1941)

About writing *Ulysses*, letter, 24 June 1921

PAINTERS HAVE OFTEN TAUGHT WRITERS HOW TO SEE. AND ONCE YOU'VE HAD THAT EXPERIENCE, YOU SEE DIFFERENTLY.

James Baldwin (1924–87)

Jordan Elgrably, 'James Baldwin, The Art of Fiction No. 78', *The Paris Review*, Spring 1984

REALLY GREAT PEOPLE ALWAYS SEE THE BEST IN OTHERS; IT IS THE LITTLE MAN WHO LOOKS FOR THE WORST—AND FINDS IT.

Samuel Coleridge-Taylor (1875–1912)

Quoted in Peter Fryer, *Staying Power: The History of Black People in Britain* (1986)

Pessimism

Nothing makes me more pessimistic than the obligation not to be pessimistic.
Eugène Ionesco (1909–94)

It is not possible for a poet...to protect himself from the tragic elements in human life...Illness, old age, and death—subjects as ancient as humanity—these are the subjects that the poet must speak of very nearly from the first moment that he begins to speak.
Louise Bogan (1897–1970)
Selected Criticism (1958)

Plagiarism

If you steal from one book you are condemned as a plagiarist, but if you steal from ten books you are considered a scholar, and if you steal from thirty or forty books, a distinguished scholar.
Amos Oz (1939–2018)

Immature poets imitate; mature poets steal.
T. S. Eliot (1888–1965)
'Philip Massinger', *The Sacred Wood* (1920)

We can say nothing but what hath been said. Our poets steal from Homer...Our story-dressers do as much; he that comes last is commonly best.

Robert Burton (1577–1640)

'Democritus to the Reader', *The Anatomy of Melancholy* (1621)

They lard their lean books with the fat of others' works.

Robert Burton (1577–1640)

'Democritus to the Reader', *The Anatomy of Melancholy* (1621)

We prefer to believe that the absence of inverted commas guarantees the originality of a thought, whereas it may be merely that the utterer has forgotten its source.

Clifton Fadiman (1904–99)

Any Number Can Play (1957)

Be careful not to copy other writers, even by accident – just read and learn.

Susan Hill (b. 1942)

Writers' & Artists' Yearbook (2014)

When you steal from one author, it's plagiarism; if you steal from many, it's research.

Wilson Mizner (1876–1933)

Quoted in Alva Johnston, *The Legendary Mizners* (2002)

P

Formerly, whenever an American film scored an outstanding success, some elderly lady would get up and claim that it plagiarised her rejected MS.

Robert Stevenson (1905–86)
Writers' & Artists' Yearbook (1933)

Plays

Plays may be written from three starting-points: Theme, Character, Plot.

A. A. Milne (1882–1956)
Writers' & Artists' Yearbook (1933)

I'm not good at precise, coherent argument. But plays are suited to incoherent argument, put into the mouths of fallible people.

Alan Bennett (b. 1934)
Sunday Times, 24 November 1991

I'm not a theorist. I'm not an authoritative or reliable commentator on the dramatic scene, the social scene, any scene. I write plays, when I can manage it, and that's all.

Harold Pinter (1930–2008)
Speech addressed to the National Student Drama Festival, Bristol, 1962

P

Pleasure

Reading is always a good way to define pleasure anew.
Richard Ford (b. 1944)
'Introduction', *The Granta Book of the Long Story* (1998)

The aristocratic pleasure of displeasing is not the only
delight that bad taste can yield. One can love a certain
kind of vulgarity for its own sake.
Aldous Huxley (1894–1963)
'Vulgarity in Literature', *Music at Night And Other Essays* (1949)

Even when poetry has a meaning, as it usually has, it may
be inadvisable to draw it out...Perfect understanding will
sometimes almost extinguish pleasure.
A. E. Housman (1859–1936)
Leslie Stephen Lecture, University of Cambridge, 9 May 1933

First, I did it for my own pleasure. Then I did it for the
pleasure of my friends. And now—I do it for money.
Ferenc Molnár (1878–1952)
George Jean Nathan, *The Intimate Notebooks of George Jean Nathan* (1932)

Poetry

Things in poetry should, I think,
Be out of place, not tidy, everyday.
Anna Akhmatova (1888–1966)
Quoted in Lydia Chukovskaya (ed.), *The Akhmatova Journals: 1938–1941, Vol. 1* (1994)

I dare not alter these things; they come to me from above.
Alfred Austin (1835–1913)
When accused of writing ungrammatical verse
Edward Marsh, *A Number of People: A Book of Reminiscences* (1939)

Poetic licence. There's no such thing.
Théodore de Banville (1823–91)
Petit traité de poésie française (1872)

I have nothing to say and I am saying it and that is poetry.
John Cage (1912–92)
Silence: Lectures and Writings (1961)

I would define the poetic effect as the capacity that a text
displays for continuing to generate different readings,
without ever being completely consumed.
Umberto Eco (1932–2016)
'Telling the Process', *Postscript to the Name of the Rose* (1983)

WRITING FREE VERSE IS LIKE PLAYING TENNIS WITH THE NET DOWN.

Robert Frost (1874–1963)

Speech at the Milton Academy, 17 May 1935

VERSE LIBRE; A DEVICE FOR MAKING POETRY EASIER TO READ AND HARDER TO WRITE.

H. L. Mencken (1880–1956)

A Book of Burlesques (1916)

P

Poetry, 'The Cinderella of the Arts'.
Harriet Monroe (1860–1936)
Quoted in Hope Stoddard, 'Harriet Monroe', *Famous American Women* (1970)

It is as unseeing to ask what is the *use* of poetry as it would be to ask what is the use of religion.
Edith Sitwell (1887–1964)
'Preface', *The Outcasts* (1962)

If Poetry comes not as naturally as Leaves to a tree it had better not come at all.
John Keats (1795–1821)
Letter to John Taylor, 27 February 1818
H. E. Rollins (ed.), *Letters of John Keats, Vol. 1* (1958)

Poem me no poems.
Rose Macaulay (1881–1958)
Poetry Review, Autumn 1963

Poetry versus prose

Poetry is to prose as dancing is to walking.
John Wain (1925–94)
Remark on BBC Radio, 13 January 1976

I wish our clever young poets would remember my homely definitions of prose and poetry; that is, prose = words in their best order;—poetry = the *best* words in the best order.

Samuel Taylor Coleridge (1772–1834)

Specimens of the Table Talk of the late Samuel Taylor Coleridge (1835)

Yea, marry, now it is somewhat, for now it is rhyme; before, it was neither rhyme nor reason.

Thomas More (1478–1535)

Quoted in Francis Bacon, *Apophthegms New and Old* (1625)

The poet gives us his essence, but prose takes the mould of the body and mind entire.

Virginia Woolf (1882–1941)

'Reading', *The Captain's Death Bed* (1950)

It may be safely affirmed, that there neither is, nor can be, any *essential* difference between the language of prose and metrical composition.

William Wordsworth (1770–1850)

'Preface', *Lyrical Ballads* (1800)

Poetry is not the proper antithesis to prose, but to science. Poetry is opposed to science, and prose to metre.

Samuel Taylor Coleridge (1772–1834)

'Lecture 1', *Lectures and Notes of 1818* (1818).

A TRUE POET DOES NOT BOTHER TO BE POETICAL. NOR DOES A NURSERY GARDENER SCENT HIS ROSES.

Jean Cocteau (1889–1963)
Professional Secrets (1922)

A POET IS NOT A PUBLIC FIGURE. A POET SHOULD BE READ AND NOT SEEN.

Cecil Day-Lewis (1904–72)
'Sayings of the Week', *Observer*, 7 January 1968

Poets

The poet lives by exaggeration and makes himself known through misunderstandings.
> **Elias Canetti** (1905–94)
> *The Agony of Flies: Notes and Notations* (1992)

The poet...like the lover...is a person unable to reconcile what he knows with what he feels. His peculiarity is that he is under a certain compulsion to do so.
> **Babette Deutsch** (1895–1982)
> 'Poetry at the Mid-Century', *The Writer's Book* (1950)

For a good poet's made, as well as born.
> **Ben Jonson** (1572–1637)

The poet begins where the man ends. The man's lot is to live his human life, the poet's to invent what is nonexistent.
> **José Ortega y Gasset** (1883–1955)
> *The Dehumanization of Art and Other Essays on Art, Culture, and Literature* (1968)

The poet is the priest of the invisible.
> **Wallace Stevens** (1879–1955)
> 'Adagia', *Opus Posthumous* (1957)

Well, of course, as a poet I would say [...] everything should be able to come into a poem, but I can't put toothbrushes into a poem, I really can't!

Slyvia Plath (1932–63)

Remark made during a recorded interview with Peter Orr
Recorded by The British Council, 30 October 1962

Point of view

The first person is the most terrifying view of all [...] the reader has no reason to trust—why should you need this I?

James Baldwin (1924–87)

Jordan Elgrably, 'James Baldwin, The Art of Fiction No. 78', *The Paris Review*, Spring 1984

I discovered, much to my surprise—and particularly if I was writing in the first person—that I could become a psychopath quite easily. [...] So I probably gave up a flourishing, lucrative career as a mass murderer.

Robert Bloch (1917–94)

Douglas E. Winters, *Bloch in Faces of Fear: Encounters With the Creators of Modern Horror* (1985)

Style is the perfection of a point of view.

Richard Eberhart (1904–2005)

Power

When power narrows the areas of man's concern, poetry reminds him of the richness and diversity of his existence.
John F. Kennedy (1917–63)
Address at the Dedication of the Robert Frost Library, 26 October 1963

All that is literature seeks to communicate power; all that is not literature, to communicate knowledge.
Thomas De Quincey (1785–1859)
'Letters to a Young Man Whose Education has been Neglected', *London Magazine*, No. 3, 1823

How does the poet speak to men with power, but by being still more a man than they?
Thomas Carlyle (1795–1881)
'Burns', *Edinburgh Review*, 1828

Praise

In recommending a book to a friend the less said the better. The moment you praise a book too highly you awaken resistance in your listener.
Henry Miller (1891–1980)
The Books in My Life (1952)

P

Praise and blame are much the same for the writer. One is better for your vanity, but neither gets you much further with your work.

Jeanette Winterson (b. 1959)
The *Guardian*, 18 June 1994

Unless a reviewer has the courage to give you unqualified praise, I say ignore the bastard.

John Steinbeck (1902–68)
John Kenneth Galbraith, 'Introduction', *The Affluent Society*

These poems, with all their crudities, doubts, and confusions, are written for the love of Man and in praise of God, and I'd be a damn' fool if they weren't.

Dylan Thomas (1914–53)
'Author's note', *Collected Poems 1934-1952* (1953)

Procrastination

No task is a long one but the task on which one dare not start. It becomes a nightmare.

Charles Baudelaire (1821–67)
'Mon Coeur mis à nu', *Journaux intimes* (1887)

The more circumspectly you delay writing down an idea, the more maturely developed it will be on surrendering itself.

Walter Benjamin (1892–1940)
Reflections: Essays, Aphorisms, Autobiographical Writings (2000)

It is not real work unless you would rather be doing something else.

J. M. Barrie (1860–1937)

Rectorial address, St. Andrews University, 3 May 1922

I was so long writing my review that I never got around to reading the book.

Groucho Marx (1890–1977)

Prose

It has been said that good prose should resemble the conversation of a well-bred man.

W. Somerset Maugham (1874–1965)

The Summing Up (1938)

Work on good prose has three steps: a musical stage when it is composed, an architectonic one when it is built, and a textile one when it is woven.

Walter Benjamin (1892–1940)

One-Way Street (1928)

Good prose should be transparent, like a window pane.

George Orwell (1903–50)

'Why I Write', *Gangrel*, Summer 1946

Publication

When a new book is published, read an old one.
   Samuel Rogers (1763–1855)

My own motto is publish and be sued.
   Richard Ingrams (b. 1937)
   Remark on BBC Radio, 4 May 1977

I tell my students that the odds of their getting published
and of it bringing them financial security, peace of mind,
and even joy are probably not that great. Ruin, hysteria,
bad skin, unsightly tics, ugly financial problems, maybe;
but probably not peace of mind.
   Anne Lamott (b. 1954)
   Bird by Bird: Some Instructions on Writing and Life (1995)

Becoming a published writer doesn't suddenly relieve you
of the process of trial and error.
   Téa Obreht (b. 1985)
   Kerri Jarema, '5 Authors On Beating The Dreaded "Second Book Syndrome"',
   Bustle, 13 November 2019

It is easy to become a publisher, but difficult to remain
one; the mortality rate in infancy is higher than in any
other trade or profession.
   Stanley Unwin (1884–1968)
   Writers' & Artists' Yearbook (1950)

Purpose

As I begin a novel I remind myself as ever of Camus's admonition that the purpose of a writer is to keep civilization from destroying itself. And even while thinking, well, fat chance! I find courage.

Fay Weldon (b. 1931)

Joe Fassler, 'Imagine Sisyphus Happy: How Camus Helps Fay Weldon Keep on Writing', *The Atlantic*, 26 February 2013

If the creator had a purpose in equipping us with a neck, he surely meant us to stick it out.

Arthur Koestler (1905–83)

Encounter, May 1970

The novel is an art form and when you use it for anything other than art, you pervert it...If you manage to use it successfully for social, religious, or other purposes, it is because you make it art first.

Flannery O'Connor (1925–64)

Letter to Father John McCown, 9 May 1956

Quality

Learn to write well, or not to write at all.
John Sheffield (1647–1721)
Essay on Satire (1680)

You are going to get things wrong. None of us mean to,
but we do.
Bernard Cornwell (b. 1944)
Writers' & Artists' Yearbook (2006)

There is an impression abroad that everyone has it in him
to write one book; but if by this is implied a good book
the impression is false.
W. Somerset Maugham (1874–1965)
The Summing Up (1938)

How clear, serene, and solid the best work still seems; it's
as if there were a physical communion taking place among
the fingers turning the page, the eyes taking in the words,
the brain imaginatively recreating what the words stand
for and, as Hemingway put it, "making it part of your
experience".
Raymond Carver (1938–88)
'Coming of Age, Going to Pieces', *No Heroics, Please* (1992)

Q

Quotations

It is a good thing for an uneducated man to read books of quotations.

Winston Churchill (1874–1965)
My Early Life (1930)

There is always the option of being emotionally lazy, that is, of quoting.

Alain de Botton (b. 1969)
Essays in Love (1994)

Did you ever read my words, or did you merely finger through them for quotations which you thought might valuably support an already conceived idea concerning some old and distorted connection between us?

Audre Lorde (1934–92)
On the erasure of black women in Mary Daly's work
An Open Letter to Mary Daly (1979)

My God, what a clumsy *olla putrida* James Joyce is! Nothing but old fags and cabbage stumps of quotations from the Bible and the rest, stewed in the juice of deliberate, journalistic dirty-mindedness.

D. H. Lawrence (1885–1930)
Letter to Aldous Huxley, 15 August 1928

WRITING TENDS TO BE VERY DELIBERATE. A NOVELIST COULD PROBABLY RUN A MILITARY CAMPAIGN WITH SOME SUCCESS. THEY COULD CERTAINLY RUN A COUNTRY.

Colm Tóibín (b. 1955)

Laura Barnett, 'Colm Tóibín, novelist—portrait of the artist', the *Guardian*, 19 February 2013

R

Readable books

At last, an unprintable book that is readable.
Ezra Pound (1885–1972)
A remark about Henry Miller's *Tropic of Cancer* (1934)

If a book is worth reading, it is worth buying.
John Ruskin (1819–1900)
'Of Kings' Treasuries', *Sesame and Lilies* (1865)

Reader

Any novel is hopeful in that it presupposes a reader.
Margaret Atwood (b. 1939)
Erica Wagner, '"Writing is always an act of hope": Margaret Atwood on *The Testaments*', *The New Statesman*, 18 September 2019

Try to read your own work as if you didn't write it – as if you are a reader coming to it for the first time.
David Lodge (b. 1935)
Foreword to *Writers' & Artists' Yearbook* (2017)

I am a writer because I'm a reader.
Mark Billingham (b. 1961)
Writers' & Artists' Yearbook (2006)

R

A poem is energy transferred from where the poet got it...by way of the poem itself to, all the way over to, the reader.

Charles Olson (1910–70)

Quoted in Nina Baym (ed.), *Norton Anthology of American Literature*

Hypocrite reader—my likeness—my brother.

Charles Baudelaire (1821–67)

'Au Lecteur', *Les Fleurs du mal* (1857)

Reading

Read not to contradict and confute, nor to believe and take for granted, nor to find talk and discourse, but to weigh and consider.

Francis Bacon (1561–1626)

'Of Studies', *Essays* (1625)

He has only half learned the art of reading who has not added to it the even more refined accomplishments of skipping and skimming.

Arthur Balfour (1848–1930)

Quoted in E. T. Raymond, *Mr. Balfour* (1920)

The reading of all good books is like a conversation with the finest men of past centuries.
René Descartes (1596–1650)
Discourse on Method (1637)

The writer is careful of what he reads, for that is what he will write. He is careful of what he learns, because that is what he will know.
Annie Dillard (b. 1945)
The Writing Life (1989)

Read in order to live.
Gustave Flaubert (1821–80)
Letter to Mademoiselle Leroyer de Chantepie, 1857

The art of reading is to skip judiciously.
Philip Gilbert Hamerton (1834–94)
The Intellectual Life (1873)

People say that life is the thing, but I prefer reading.
Logan Pearsall Smith (1865–1946)
'Myself', *Afterthoughts* (1931)

Let's be reasonable and add an eighth day to the week that is devoted exclusively to reading.
Lena Dunham (b. 1986)
Posted on Twitter, 28 April 2013

R

Reading—I discovered—comes before writing. A society can exist—many do exist—without writing, but no society can exist without reading.

Alberto Manguel (b. 1948)
'The Last Page', *A History of Reading* (1996)

To read too many books is harmful.

Mao Zedong (1893–1976)
New Yorker, 7 March 1977

There was a time when the average reader read a novel simply for the moral he could get out of it, and however naïve that may have been, it was a good deal less naïve than some of the limited objectives he has now.

Flannery O'Connor (1925–64)
Lecture, Wesleyan College, Macon, Georgia (1960)

Reading, to me, is simply the expansion of one's mind to include some people whom you just didn't get to meet before.

Ntozake Shange (1948–2018)
Quoted in Claudia Tate (ed.), *Black Women Writers at Work* (1983)

Reading maketh a full man; conference a ready man; and writing an exact man.

Francis Bacon (1561–1626)
'Of Studies', *Essays* (1625)

HAVE REGRETS. THEY ARE FUEL. ON THE PAGE THEY FLARE INTO DESIRE.

Geoff Dyer (b. 1958)

'Ten rules for writing fiction', the *Guardian*, 20 February 2010

———————————

Rejection

You have to know how to accept rejection and reject acceptance.

Ray Bradbury (1920–2012)

Remark on WAMU Radio station, 5 April 1995, Washington D.C.

No editor can ever afford the rejection of a good thing, and no author the publication of a bad one. The only difficulty lies in drawing the line.

Thomas Wentworth Higginson (1823–1911)

'A Letter to a Young Contributor', *The Atlantic Monthly*, Spring 1862

Anyway, if you don't like someone's story, you write your own.

Chinua Achebe (1930–2013)

Jerome Brooks, 'Chinua Achebe, The Art of Fiction No. 139', *The Paris Review*, Winter 1994

Reputation

The greatest renown today consists in being admired or hated without having been read.

Albert Camus (1913–60)

Create Dangerously (1950)

A list of authors who have made themselves most beloved and, therefore, most comfortable financially, shows that it is our national joy to mistake for the first-rate, the fecund rate.

Dorothy Parker (1893–1967)
Quoted in James R. Gaines, *Wit's End: Days and Nights of the Algonquin Round Table* (1977)

A novelist who writes nothing for 10 years finds his reputation rising. Because I keep on producing books they say there must be something wrong with this fellow.

J. B. Priestley (1894–1984)
'Sayings of the Week', *Observer*, 21 September 1969

Research

Having done the research, you must reject a great deal of it.

Bernard Cornwell (b. 1944)
Writers' & Artists' Yearbook (2006)

Do a minimum of research, and then keep it out. Don't let it impede the story.

Brian Moore (1921–99)
Rosemary Hartill, *Writers Revealed* (1989)

Research is formalized curiosity. It is poking and prying with a purpose.

Zora Neale Hurston (1891–1960)
Dust Tracks on a Road (1942)

Read, read, read. I'm not sure that one can be a good writer without being a good reader. If you're going to build a desk it's very good to see what other carpenters have done.

Chimamanda Ngozi Adichie (b. 1977)
'How To Become A Published Author; Advice From Chimamanda Ngozi Adichie', *Stylist* Book Club, 10 June 2014

Respect

There exist only three beings worthy of respect: the priest, the soldier, the poet. To know, to kill, to create.

Charles Baudelaire (1821–67)
'Mon Coeur mis à nu', *Journaux intimes* (1887)

Once I learned to value and respect my characters, I could really hear them. I let them start talking. The important thing is not to censor them.

August Wilson (1945–2005)
Bonnie Lyons & George Plimpton, 'August Wilson, The Art of Theater No. 14', *The Paris Review*, Winter 1999

Rewriting

There is no such thing as good writing, only good rewriting.

Robert Graves (1895–1985)

Joe Fassler, 'There's No Such Thing as Good Writing: Craig Nova's Radical Revising Process', *The Atlantic*, 11 June 2013

Any story that is any good, is usually going to change.

Alice Munro (b. 1931)

Jeanne McCulloch & Mona Simpson, 'Alice Munro, The Art of Fiction No. 137', *The Paris Review*, Summer 1994

[...] the second draft is where I try and make it look like I knew what I was doing all along.

Neil Gaiman (b. 1960)

The Tim Feriss Show Blog, 30 March 2019

One must write and rewrite till one writes it right.

A. R. Ammons (1926–2001)

Garbage (1993)

The book really comes to life in the rewriting.

Philip Roth (1933–2018)

R

Roads

I have never found anywhere, in the domain of art, that
you don't have to walk to [. . .] There are, or course, roads.
Great artists make the roads; good teachers and good
companions can point them out. But there ain't no free
rides, baby. No hitchhiking.

Ursula K. Le Guin (1929–2018)
The Language of the Night (1979)

A writer depicting humdrum realities is comparable to
a prophet incapable of performing miracles in which
mountains are dislodged and rivers are turned into roads.

Nuruddin Farah (b. 1945)
'In praise of exile', *Third World Affairs* (1988)

Royalties

I've always believed in writing without a collaborator,
because where two people are writing the same book, each
believes he gets all the worry and only half the royalties.

Agatha Christie (1890–1976)
Quoted in Hal Zina Bennet with Michael Larsen, *How to Write with
a Collaborator* (1988)

We who live by writing and publishing want and should demand our fair share of the proceeds; but the name of our beautiful reward isn't profit. Its name is freedom.

Ursula K. Le Guin (1929–2018)
Speech given in Acceptance of the National Book Foundation Medal, 19 November 2014

Rules

Writing can be encouraged, perhaps, but taught? To teach something implies there is something to be taught and that suggests that the activity can be reduced to, if not rules, maxims. But there are no rules except to tell a story.

Bernard Cornwell (b. 1944)
Writers' & Artists' Yearbook (2006)

If you're a really great writer, none of these rules need apply.

Rose Tremain (b. 1943)
'Ten rules for writing fiction (Part two)', the *Guardian*, 20 February 2010

S

Satire

Mark Twain and I are in the same position. We have to put things in such a way as to make people, who would otherwise hang us, believe that we are joking.
   George Bernard Shaw (1856–1950)

It is disappointing to report that George Bernard Shaw appearing as George Bernard Shaw is sadly miscast in the part. Satirists should be heard and not seen.
   Robert E. Sherwood (1896–1955)

Only mediocrity can be trusted to be always at its best.
   Max Beerbohm (1872–1956)
   S. N. Behrman, *Conversations with Max* (1960)

No poet or novelist wishes he were the only one who ever lived, but most of them wish they were the only one alive, and quite a number fondly believe their wish has been granted.
   W. H. Auden (1907–73)
   'Writing', *The Dyer's Hand* (1963)

S

Science

If Galileo had said in verse that the world moved, the Inquisition might have let him alone.
Thomas Hardy (1840–1928)
Quoted in Florence Hardy, *The Later Years of Thomas Hardy, 1892–1928* (1930)

To speak algebraically, Mr. M. is execrable, but Mr. C. is $(x + 1)$-ecrable.
Edgar Allan Poe (1809–49)
Referring to the writers Cornelius Mathews and William Ellery Channing
Quoted in N. Rose, *Mathematical Maxims and Minims* (1988)

All one's inventions are true, you can be sure of that. Poetry is as exact a science as geometry.
Gustave Flaubert (1821–80)
Letter to Louise Colet, 14 August 1853
Quoted in M. Nadeau (ed.), *Correspondence, 1853–56* (1964)

Science fiction

Science fiction is no more written for scientists than ghost stories are written for ghosts.
Brian Aldiss (1925–2017)
'Introduction', *The Penguin Science Fiction Omnibus* (1973)

Science fiction is the search for a definition of mankind and his status in the universe which will stand in our advanced but confused state of knowledge (science), and is characteristically cast in the Gothic or post-Gothic mode.

Brian Aldiss (1925–2017)
Trillion Year Spree (1986)

Science fiction writers, I am sorry to say, really do not know anything. We can't talk about science, because our knowledge of it is limited and unofficial, and usually our fiction is dreadful.

Philip K. Dick (1928–82)
'How to Build a Universe That Doesn't Fall Apart Two Days Later',
Playboy (1980)

Self-knowledge

The most difficult secret for a man to keep is his own opinion of himself.

Marcel Pagnol (1895–1974)
Remark made 15 March 1954

S

Self-knowledge is a dangerous thing, tending to make man shallow or insane.

Karl Shapiro (1913–2000)
The Bourgeois Poet (1964)

The most essential gift for any writer is a built-in, shock-proof, shit detector. This is the writer's radar and all great writers have had it.

Ernest Hemingway (1899–1961)
George Plimpton, 'Ernest Hemingway, The Art of Fiction No. 21', *The Paris Review*, Spring 1958

There's nothing worse than the writer who learns to do something and then goes on doing it because it's comfortable and safe. It is a gift of wings, and you learn to trust yourself, that you will not fall—or if you do, that you will just swoop up again.

Jeanette Winterson (b. 1959)
The *Guardian*, 18 June 1994

Sentences

Be ship-shape. An ocean liner might be big, but all the screws need to be tight. Or you end up drowning. So, y'know, observe each sentence as if it was the only one.

Matt Haig (b. 1975)
'25 rules for writing a novel', *BookTrust*

I really do not know that anything has ever been more exciting than diagramming sentences.

Gertrude Stein (1874–1946)

Lectures in America (1935)

When it comes right down to it, nothing has changed. The English sentence is just as difficult to write as it ever was.

John Steinbeck (1902–68)

Remark following his 1962 Nobel Prize in Literature

Whatever sentence will bear to be read twice, we may be sure was thought twice.

Henry David Thoreau (1817–62)

The Writings of Henry David Thoreau (1894)

Sentences which simply express moral judgements do not say anything. They are pure expressions of feeling and as such do not come under the category of truth and falsehood.

A. J. Ayer (1910–89)

Language, Truth and Logic (1936)

The most attractive sentences are not perhaps the wisest, but the surest and soundest.

Henry David Thoreau (1817–1862)

Robert Sattelmeyer (ed.), *The Writings of Henry David Thoreau: Journal, Volume 2: 1842–1848* (1984)

S

Sentimentality

Sentimentality is the emotional promiscuity of those who have no sentiment.

Norman Mailer (1923–2007)

Cannibals and Christians (1966)

Sentimentality is only sentiment that rubs you up the wrong way.

W. Somerset Maugham (1874–1965)

A Writer's Notebook (1949)

Sex

A writer is a writer, and writing is sexless.

Buchi Emecheta (1944–2017)

Adeola James, 'Buchi Emecheta' [Interview], *In Their Own Voices: African Women Writers Talk* (1990)

My criterion for writing a sex scene is, Do people know more about this character, having gone through this scene with them, than they did when they started?

Pat Barker (b. 1943)

Valerie Stivers, 'Pat Barker, The Art of Fiction No. 243', *The Paris Review*, Winter 2018

God forbid people should read our books to find the juicy passages.

Graham Greene (1904–91)

'Sayings of the Week', *Observer*, 14 October 1979

I am compulsive about writing, I need to do it the way I need sleep and exercise and food and sex.

John Irving (b. 1942)

Ron Hansen, 'John Irving, The Art of Fiction No. 93', *The Paris Review*, Summer-Fall 1986

I can't understand these chaps who go round American universities explaining how they write poems: It's like going round explaining how you sleep with your wife.

Philip Larkin (1922–85)

Robert Phillips, 'Philip Larkin, The Art of Poetry No. 30', *The Paris Review*, Summer 1982

It is the sexless novel that should be distinguished: the sex novel is now normal.

George Bernard Shaw (1856–1950)

Table-Talk of G. B. S. (1925)

His excessive emphasis on sex was due to the fact that in sex alone he was compelled to admit that he was not the only human being in the universe.

Bertrand Russell (1872–1970)

The Autobiography of Bertrand Russell, 1914–1944, Vol 2 (1968)

S

As in the sexual experience, there are never more than two persons present in the act of reading—the writer who is the impregnator, and the reader who is the respondent.

E. B. White (1899–1985)
The Second Tree from the Corner (1954)

The few bad poems which occasionally are created during abstinence are of no great interest.

Wilhelm Reich (1897–1957)
Theodore P. Wolfe (trans.), *The Sexual Revolution* (1945)

Short stories

In its earlier phases storytelling, like poetry and drama, was a public art...But the short story, like the novel, is a modern art form; that is to say, it represents, better than poetry or drama, our own attitude to life.

Frank O'Connor (1903–66)
'Introduction', *The Lonely Voice: A Study of the Short Story* (1962)

A novel is a river, but a short story is a glass of water. A novel is a forest, but the short story is a seed. It is more atomic. The atom may contain the secret structures of the universe.

Ben Okri (b. 1959)
Quoted in Jane Wilkinson, *Talking with African Writers* (1992)

WRITING SAVED ME FROM THE SIN AND INCONVENIENCE OF VIOLENCE.

Alice Walker (b. 1944)

'One Child of One's Own', *Ms*, August 1979

———————————

IF TWITTER OR FACEBOOK IS THE ANSWER, IT'S PROBABLY THE WRONG QUESTION.

Ben Schott (b. 1974)

Writers' & Artists' Yearbook (2015)

———————————

S

Soul

A good book is the purest essence of a human soul.
Thomas Carlyle (1795–1881)
Speech given in 1840 in support of the London Library
Quoted in F. Harrison, *Carlyle and the London Library* (1907)

Poetry should be great and unobtrusive, a thing which enters into one's soul, and does not startle or amaze it with itself, but with its subject.
John Keats (1795–1821)
Letter to John Hamilton Reynolds, 3 February 1818
H. E. Rollins (ed.), *Letters of John Keats, Vol. 1* (1958)

I believe the souls of five hundred Sir Isaac Newtons would go to the making up of a Shakespeare or a Milton.
Samuel Taylor Coleridge (1772–1834)
Letter to Thomas Poole, 23 March 1801

The difference between genuine poetry and the poetry of Dryden, Pope, and all their school, is briefly this: their poetry is conceived and composed in their wits, genuine poetry is conceived and composed in the soul.
Matthew Arnold (1822–88)
'Thomas Gray', *Essays in Criticism, Second Series* (1888)

Most people sell their souls, and live with a good conscience on the proceeds.

Logan Pearsall Smith (1865–1946)
'Other people', *Afterthoughts* (1931)

Speech

The true use of speech is not so much to express our wants as to conceal them.

Oliver Goldsmith (1728–74)
'The Use of Language', *Essays* (1765)

A conversation is a dialogue, not a monologue. That's why there are so few good conversations: due to scarcity, two intelligent talkers seldom meet.

Truman Capote (1924–84)
Cathleen Medwick, 'Truman Capote: An Interview, *Vogue*, December 1979

Talking and eloquence are not the same: to speak, and to speak well, are two things.

Ben Jonson (1572–1637)
Timber, or, Discoveries Made upon Men and Matter (1640)

Writing is a way of talking without being interrupted.

Jules Renard (1864–1910)
Journal, 1877-1910

S

Speeches

I take the view, and always have done, that if you cannot say what you have to say in twenty minutes, you should go away and write a book about it.
   Derek Brabazon (1910–74)

A good indignation makes an excellent speech.
   Ralph Waldo Emerson (1803–82)
   Letters and Social Aims (1886)

Why doesn't the fellow who says, "I'm no speechmaker", let it go at that instead of giving a demonstration.
   Frank McKinney Hubbard (1868–1930)

It usually takes more than three weeks to prepare a good impromptu speech.
   Mark Twain (1835–1910)

Spontaneity

Away with all ideals. Let each individual act spontaneously from the for ever incalculable prompting of the creative wellhead within him. There is no universal law.
   D. H. Lawrence (1885–1930)
   'Preface', *All Things Are Possible* (1920)

The one and only basis of the moral life must be spontaneity, that is, the immediate, the unreflective.

Jean-Paul Sartre (1905–80)

Notebooks for an Ethics (1983)

Struggle

I begin already to weigh my words and sentences more than I did, and am looking about for a sentiment, an illustration or a metaphor in every corner of the room.

Jane Austen (1775–1817)

Letter to her sister Cassandra, 1809

Out of the quarrel with others we make rhetoric; out of the quarrel with ourselves we make poetry.

W. B. Yeats (1865–1939)

'Anima Hominus', *Essays* (1924)

Even when passages seemed to come easily, as though I were copying from a folio held open by smiling angels, the manuscript revealed the usual signs of struggle— bloodstains, teethmarks, gashes, and burns.

Annie Dillard (b. 1945)

The Writing Life (1989)

The great struggle of a writer is to learn to write as he would talk.

Lincoln Steffens (1866–1936)

Justin Kaplan, *Lincoln Steffens: Portrait of a Great American Journalist* (2013)

Stupidity

To generalize is to be an idiot.

William Blake (1757–1827)

Annotation written on a copy of Sir Joshua Reynolds's *Discourses* (1778)

Quoted in Alexander Gilchrist, *Life of Blake* (1942)

Even stupidity is the product of highly organized matter.

Milan Kundera (b. 1929)

Quoted in Miroslav Holub, *Shedding Life* (1997)

My loathings are simple: stupidity, oppression, crime, cruelty, soft music.

Vladimir Nabokov (1899–1977)

Style

Style is a simple way of saying complicated things.

Jean Cocteau (1889–1963)

Le Secret professionnel (1924)

An author arrives at a good style when his language performs what is required of it without shyness.
Cyril Connolly (1903–74)
Enemies of Promise (1938)

It is the beginning of the end when you discover you have style.
Dashiell Hammett (1894–1961)
James Cooper, 'Lean Years for the Thin Man', the *Washington Daily News*, 11 March 1957

Proper words in proper places, make the true definition of a style.
Jonathan Swift (1667–1745)
A Letter To A Young Gentleman, Lately Enter'd Into Holy Orders (1720)

The writer's style is his doppelgänger, an apparition that the writer must never trust to do his work for him.
Joy Williams (b. 1944)
Will Blythe (ed.), *In Why I Write: Thoughts on the Craft of Fiction* (1998)

The true writer has nothing to say, just a way of saying it.
Alain Robbe-Grillet (1922–2008)
Pour un nouveau roman (1963)

Submission

[...] but if you ask yourself if it's unbearable, you find
yourself preparing the next self-addressed stamped
envelope pretty quickly.
Jessica Francis Kane
Joe Fassler, 'Marcus Aurelius's One Question to Beat Procrastination, Whining,
and Struggle', *The Atlantic*, 28 May 2013

Don't stuff your manuscript into an envelope as soon as
you've written 'The End'. You owe it to yourself to get the
script into the best possible state before anyone sees it.
Lee Hall (b. 1966)
Writers' & Artists' Yearbook (1998)

Success

The last thing a human who spends their day selling home
insurance in an office that smells of egg sandwiches and
despair wants to hear is that their old school friend is
going to be an international bestselling author.
Matt Haig (b. 1975)
'25 rules for writing a novel', *BookTrust*

I detest and despise success, yet I cannot do without it. I am like a drug addict if nobody talks about me for a couple of months I have withdrawal symptoms.

Eugène Ionesco (1909–94)

Shusha Guppy, 'Eugene Ionesco, The Art of Theater No. 6', *The Paris Review*, Fall 1984

Poetry isn't a kind of paint-spray you use to cover selected objects with. A good poem about failure is a success.

Philip Larkin (1922–85)

Robert Phillips, 'Philip Larkin, The Art of Poetry No. 30', *The Paris Review*, Summer 1982

Superiority

I am a man, and alive...For this reason I am a novelist. And being a novelist, I consider myself superior to the saint, the scientist, the philosopher, and the poet, who are all great masters of different bits of man alive, but never get the whole hog.

D. H. Lawrence (1885–1930)

'Why the Novel Matters', *Phoenix* (1929)

He was his own greatest invention.

John Osborne (1929–94)

Referring to Noël Coward

Talent

There is nothing new in art except talent.
Anton Chekhov (1860–1904)
Quoted in Camille Jordan, Leon Levenson & Rosemary Holsinger, *The Creative Encounter* (1971)

Talent alone cannot make a writer. There must be a man behind the book.
Ralph Waldo Emerson (1803–82)
'Goethe; or, the writer', *Representative Men* (1850)

I cannot write as well as some people; my talent is in coming up with good stories about lawyers. That is what I am good at.
John Grisham (b. 1955)
Independent on Sunday, 5 June 1994

Literature is an occupation in which you have to keep proving your talent to people who have none.
Jules Renard (1864–1910)
The Journal of Jules Renard (2008)

The most important thing for me is that I've used my talents as a writer to enable the Ogoni people to confront their tormentors. I was not able to do it as a politician or a businessman. My writing did it.

Ken Saro-Wiwa (1941–95)
Letter to William Boyd
A Month and a Day: A Detention Diary (1995)

Taste

Good taste is better than bad taste, but bad taste is better than no taste.

Arnold Bennett (1867–1931)
'Sayings of the Week', *Observer*, 24 August 1930

If you like my novels, I commend your good taste.

Rita Mae Brown (b. 1944)
'Author's Note', *Southern Discomfort* (1982)

It is the wishes and likings of the mass which largely dictate what the rest of us shall see and hear.

Stephen Leacock (1869–1944)
Humour: Its Theory and Technique (1935)

THE KIND OF PEOPLE WHO ALWAYS GO ON ABOUT WHETHER A THING IS IN GOOD TASTE INVARIABLY HAVE VERY BAD TASTE.

Joe Orton (1933–67)

'Joe Orton interviewed by Giles Gordon', *Transatlantic Review*, No. 24, Spring 1967

WRITERS, LIKE TEETH, ARE DIVIDED INTO INCISORS AND GRINDERS.

Walter Bagehot (1826–77)

'The First Edinburgh Reviewers', *Estimates of Some Englishmen and Scotchmen* (1858)

Technique

So sometimes the critic will say, 'Maya Angelou has a new book and it's very good, but then she's a natural writer.' Well, being a natural writer is like being a natural open heart surgeon.

Maya Angelou (1928–2014)

Melvin Mcleod, '"There's No Place to Go But Up" — bell hooks and Maya Angelou in conversation', *Shambhala Sun*, 1 January 1998

I think technique is different from craft. Craft is what you can learn from other verse...[Technique] involves the discovery of ways to go out of...normal cognitive bounds and raid in the inarticulate.

Seamus Heaney (1939–2013)

'Feeling into Words', *Preoccupations: Selected Prose 1968-1978* (1980)

Byron's technique is rotten.

Ezra Pound (1885–1972)

Letter to Iris Barry, 27 July 1916
D. D. Paige (ed.), *The Letters of Ezra Pound, 1907–1941* (1950)

Every writer has compressed time and procedure [...] That's not a scandal: it's a legitimate dramatic technique.

Chris Chibnall (b. 1970)

The *Guardian*, 4 March 2015

Time

[...] writing, for me, is like receiving a term of imprisonment—you know that's what you're in for, for whatever time it takes.

Chinua Achebe (1930–2013)

Jerome Brooks, 'Chinua Achebe, The Art of Fiction No. 139', *The Paris Review*, Winter 1994

I don't read novels whilst I'm writing one; I just haven't got a wide enough brain to concentrate on incoming and outgoing in the same time zone.

Dawn French (b. 1957)

The middle of a novel is a state of mind. Strange things happen in it. Time collapses.

Zadie Smith (b. 1975)

Changing My Mind: Occasional Essays (2009)

Ask a writer what she values most in her creative life, and she is likely to respond, "Time to write."

J. Robert Lennon

'The Truth About Writers,' *Los Angeles Times*, 21 June 2009

Translation

The original is unfaithful to the translation.
Jorge Luis Borges (1899–1986)
Referring to Samuel Henley's translation of *Vathek: An Arabian Tale* (1786) by the British writer William Beckford in 1943

Such is our pride, our folly, or our fate,
That few, but such as cannot write, translate.
John Denham (1615–69)
To Sir Richard Fanshaw, Upon his Translation of *Pastor Fido*

Poetry is what gets lost in translation. It is also what is lost in interpretation.
Robert Frost (1874–1963)
Quoted in Louis Untermeyer, *Robert Frost: A Backward Look* (1964)

The third, and worst, degree of turpitude is reached when a masterpiece is planished and patted into such a shape, vilely beautified in such a fashion as to conform to the notions and prejudices of a given public.
Vladimir Nabokov (1899–1977)
On the sins of translation
'The Art of Translation', *The New Republic*, 4 August 1941

A linguistic work translated into another language is like someone going across the border without his skin and putting on the local garb on the other side.

Karl Kraus (1874–1936)

Harry Zohn (ed.), 'Riddles and Solutions', *Half-Truths and One-And-A-Half-Truths: Selected Aphorisms* (1976)

Translating is the ultimate act of comprehending.

Alberto Manguel (b. 1948)

A History of Reading (1996)

I don't think a book properly exists in the world till it's been translated into another language from its original.

Ali Smith (b. 1962)

'The Waterstones Interview: Ali Smith', *Waterstones Blog*, 25 August 2020

An idea does not pass from one language to another without change.

Miguel de Unamuno y Jugo (1864–1936)

Tragic Sense of Life (1912)

Before you set out to translate poetry from one language to the other, you should make sure that you know at least one of the bloody languages!

Faiz Ahmed Faiz (1911–84)

Remark made to a friend and shared by his son-in-law, the playwright Shoaib Hashmi

Truth

So let great authors have their due, as time, which is the author of authors, be not deprived of his due, which is further and further to discover truth.

Francis Bacon (1561–1626)
The Advancement of Learning (1605)

Literature is a process of producing grand, beautiful, well-ordered lies that tell more truth than any assemblage of facts.

Julian Barnes (b. 1946)
Shusha Guppy, 'Julian Barnes The Art of Fiction No. 165', *The Paris Review*, Winter 2000

All the poet can do today is to warn. That is why the true Poets must be truthful.

Wilfred Owen (1893–1918)
'Preface', *Poems* (1920)

Poe gave the sense for the first time in America that literature is *serious*, not a matter of courtesy but of truth.

William Carlos Williams (1883–1963)
In the American Grain (1925)

Typewriter

Miller is not really a writer but a non-stop talker to whom someone has given a typewriter.
> **Gerald Brenan** (1894–1987)
> 'Literature', *Thoughts in a Dry Season* (1978)

I keep them [three typewriters] chiefly to remind myself I was once a writer.
> **Dashiell Hammett** (1894–1961)
> James Cooper, 'Lean Years for the Thin Man', *Washington Daily News*, 11 March 1957

I always say that you cannot tell what a picture really is or what an object really is until you dust it every day and you cannot tell what a book is until you type it or proof-read it.
> **Gertrude Stein** (1874–1946)
> *The Autobiography of Alice B. Toklas* (1933)

It's not writing, it's typing.
> **Truman Capote** (1924–84)
> Pati Hill, 'Truman Capote, The Art of Fiction No. 17', *The Paris Review*, Spring-Summer 1957

U
V

Unhappiness

Writing is not a profession but a vocation of unhappiness.

Georges Simenon (1903–89)

Carvel Collins, 'Georges Simenon, The Art of Fiction No. 9', *The Paris Review*, Summer 1955

What is a poet? A poet is an unhappy being whose heart is torn by secret sufferings, but whose lips are so strangely formed that when the sighs and the cries escape them, they sound like beautiful music.

Søren Kierkegaard (1813–55)

Either/Or (1843)

No sooner is it a little calmer with me than it is almost too calm. As though I have a true feeling of myself only when I am unbearably unhappy. That is probably true, too.

Franz Kafka (1883–1924)

The Diaries of Franz Kafka (1948)

Unreadable

This is not a novel to be tossed aside lightly. It should be thrown with great force.

Dorothy Parker (1893–1967)

Quoted in Robert E. Drennan, *The Algonquin Wits* (1968)

Gertrude Stein...is perhaps less important for her work, unreadable at times and intentionally obscure, than for her personal influence and her curious literary theories.

Jorge Luis Borges (1899–1986)
An Introduction to American Literature (1967)

Vanity

Mirrors are ices which do not melt: what melts are those who admire themselves in them.

Paul Morand (1888–1976)
'La Nuit écossaise...', *Ouvert la nuit* (1922)

To give an accurate and exhaustive account of that period would need a far less brilliant pen than mine.

Max Beerbohm (1872–1956)
The Yellow Book (1895)

Whatever talents I possess may suddenly diminish or suddenly increase. I can with ease become an ordinary fool. I may be one now. But it doesn't do to upset one's own vanity.

Dylan Thomas (1914–53)
Dylan Thomas: The Collected Letters (2014)

My novel is so terrific that I cannot put pen to paper.
Christopher Isherwood (1904–86)
Quoted in Stephen Spender, *Journals* (1985)

He would like to destroy his old diaries and to appear
before his children and the public only in his patriarchal
robes. His vanity is immense!
Sophia Tolstoy (1844–1919)
Alexander Werth (trans.), *The Diary of Tolstoy's Wife 1860-1891* (1928)

Virtues and vices

It is the restrictions placed on vice by our social code
which makes its pursuit so peculiarly agreeable.
Kenneth Grahame (1859–1932)
'Cheap knowledge', *Pagan Papers* (1893)

Curious, but we have come to a place, a time, when virtue
is no longer considered a virtue. The mention of virtue is
ridiculed, and even the word itself has fallen out of favor.
Maya Angelou (1928–2014)
'When Virtue Becomes Redundant', *Wouldn't Take Nothing for My Journey Now* (1993)

EVERYBODY WRITES A BOOK TOO MANY.

Mordecai Richler (1931–2001)
'Sayings of the Week', *Observer*, 9 January 1985

BETTER TO WRITE FOR YOURSELF AND HAVE NO PUBLIC, THAN WRITE FOR THE PUBLIC AND HAVE NO SELF.

Cyril Connolly (1903–74)
The New Statesman, 25 February 1933

The greatest offence against virtue is to speak ill of it.
   William Hazlitt (1778–1830)
   'On Cant and Hypocrisy', *Sketches and Essays* (1839)

It is the function of vice to keep virtue within reasonable bounds.
   Samuel Butler (1835–1902)
   H. Festing Jones (ed.), *The Note-Books of Samuel Butler* (1926)

The greatest minds are capable of the greatest vices as well as of the greatest virtues.
   René Descartes (1596–1650)
   Discourse on Method (1637)

W

Warfare

A young, earnest American brought up the subject of nuclear warfare which, he said might well destroy the entire human race. "I can't wait," P. G. Wodehouse murmured.

Malcolm Muggeridge (1903–90)
Tread Softly For You Tread on My Jokes (1966)

Above all I am not concerned with Poetry. My subject is War, and the pity of War. The Poetry is in the pity.

Wilfred Owen (1893–1918)
'Preface', *Poems* (1920)

If you are in difficulties with a book, try the element of surprise: attack it at an hour when it isn't expecting it.

H. G. Wells (1866–1946)

Wealth

I became so wealthy that I could afford to have pizza for dinner every night of the week if I wished, which for me, is the definition of wealth.

Caitlin Moran (b. 1975)
Anne McCarthy, 'The Ms. Q&A: Caitlin Moran Wants to Write What Needs to be Written', *Ms.*, 22 October 2018

Writing is the only profession where no one considers you ridiculous if you earn no money.

Jules Renard (1864–1910)

Journal, 1877–1910 (1925)

It is a sad fact about our culture that a poet can earn much more money writing or talking about his art than he can by practising it.

W. H. Auden (1907–73)

'Foreword', *The Dyer's Hand* (1963)

Writing is turning one's worst moments into money.

J. P. Donleavy (1926–2017)

Molly McKaughan and Fayette Hickox, 'J. P. Donleavy, The Art of Fiction No. 53', *The Paris Review*, Fall 1975

Weather

Never open a book with weather.

Elmore Leonard (1925–2013)

'Ten rules for writing fiction', the *Guardian*, 20 February 2010

All good books are alike in that they are truer than if they had really happened and after you are finished reading one you will feel that all that happened to you and afterwards it all belongs to you.

Ernest Hemingway (1899–1961)

'Old Newsman Writes', *Esquire*, December 1934

The poet may be used as the barometer, but let us not forget he is also part of the weather.

Lionel Trilling (1905–75)

'The Sense of the Past', *The Liberal Imagination* (1950)

I'd rather be a lightning rod than a seismograph.

Ken Kesey (1935–2001)

Quoted in Tom Wolfe, *The Electric Kool-aid Acid Test* (1968)

A lonesome man on a rainy day who does not know how to read.

Benjamin Franklin (1706–90)

On being asked what condition of man he considered the most pitiable

C. A. Shriner, *Wit, Wisdom and Foibles of the Great* (1920)

Whispers

There are things that get whispered about that writers are there to overhear.

Ann Beattie (b. 1947)

New York Times, 1 November 1987

What I like in a good author is not what he says but what he whispers.

Logan Pearsall Smith (1865–1946)

All Trivia (1933)

Fiction is a physical confessional: when you're within the covers of a book, you can admit to all kinds of things that you can't otherwise.

Joanna Trollope (b. 1943)

Claire Armistead, 'Joanna Trollope on families, fiction and feminism: "Society still expects women to do all the caring"', the *Guardian*, 2 March 2020

Wisdom

A wise man will make more opportunities than he finds.

Francis Bacon (1561–1626)

'Of Ceremonies and Respects', *Essays* (1625)

Our age has robbed millions of the simplicity of ignorance, and has so far failed to lift them to simplicity of wisdom.

Robertson Davies (1913–95)

A Voice from the Attic (1960)

We are wiser than we know.

Ralph Waldo Emerson (1803–82)

'The Over-Soul', *Essays* (1841)

The most fluent talkers or most plausible reasoners are not always the justest thinkers.

William Hazlitt (1778–1830)

'On Prejudice', *Sketches and Essays* (1839)

The older I grow, the more I distrust the familiar doctrine
that age brings wisdom.

H. L. Mencken (1880–1956)

Prejudices: Third Series (1922)

You must not think me necessarily foolish because I am
facetious, nor will I consider you necessarily wise because
you are grave.

Sydney Smith (1771–1845)

Letter to Bishop Blomfield, *The Times*, 5 September 1840

Wit

His foe was folly and his weapon wit.

Anthony Hope (1863–1933)

Epitaph for W. S. Gilbert, erected in 1915

However fluent or witty your prose, it is simply no longer
enough just to jump on a train.

William Dalrymple (b. 1965)

Writers' & Artists' Yearbook (2006)

Wit ought to be a glorious treat like caviar; never spread it
about like marmalade.

Noël Coward (1899–1973)

Quoted in Margaret Hainson, *Never Spread Like Marmalade* (1975)

Words

The word connects the visible trace with the invisible thing, the absent thing, the thing that is desired or feared, like a frail emergency bridge flung over an abyss.

Italo Calvino (1923–85)
'Exactitude', *Six Memos for the Next Millennium* (1988)

One must be drenched in words, literally soaked in them, to have the right ones form themselves into the proper pattern at the right moment.

Hart Crane (1899–1932)
Langdon Hammer & Brom Weber (ed.), *O my Land, My Friends: The Selected Letters of Hart Crane* (1997)

The basic tool for the manipulation of reality is the manipulation of words. If you can control the meaning of words, you can control the people who must use the words.

Philip K. Dick (1928–82)
'How to Build a Universe That Doesn't Fall Apart Two Days Later', *I Hope I Shall Arrive Soon* (1985)

YOU CAN STROKE PEOPLE WITH WORDS.

F. Scott Fitzgerald (1896–1940)

The Crack-Up: with Other Uncollected Pieces, Note-Books and Unpublished Letters (1945)

ONE FORGETS WORDS AS ONE FORGETS NAMES. ONE'S VOCABULARY NEEDS CONSTANT FERTILISATION OR IT WILL DIE.

Evelyn Waugh (1903–66)

Michael Davie (ed.), *Diaries of Evelyn Waugh* (1976)

W

The arrow belongs not to the archer when it has once left the bow; the word no longer belongs to the speaker when it has once passed his lips.

Heinrich Heine (1797–1856)

'Preface', *Religion and Philosophy in Germany* (1852, second edition)

There aren't any new words. Our job is to give new meanings and special overtones to absolutely ordinary words.

Haruki Murakami (b. 1949)

'Jazz Messenger', *The New York Times*, 6 July 2007

The English language is full of words that are just waiting to be misspelled, and the world is full of sticklers, ready to pounce.

Mary Norris (b. 1952)

Between You & Me: Confessions of a Comma Queen (2015)

Unless you are writing something very post-modernist – self-conscious, self-reflexive and "provocative" – be alert for possibilities of using plain familiar words in place of polysyllabic "big" words.

Joyce Carol Oates (b. 1938)

'Ten rules for writing fiction (Part two)', the *Guardian*, 20 February 2010

You don't make a poem with thoughts; you must make it with words.

Jean Cocteau (1889–1963)
Sunday Times, 20 October 1963

Until we learn the use of living words we shall continue to be waxworks inhabited by gramophones.

Walter de la Mare (1873–1956)
'Sayings of the Week', *Observer*, 12 May 1929

Writers are ...

Writers are always selling somebody out.

Joan Didion (b. 1934)
'Preface', *Slouching Towards Bethlehem* (1968)

The writer isn't made in a vacuum. Writers are witnesses. The reason we need writers is because we need witnesses to this terrifying century.

E. L. Doctorow (1931–2015)
George Plimpton, 'The Art of Fiction No. 94', *The Paris Review*, Winter 1986

A writer is a person who writes.

John Braine (1922–86)
How to Write a Novel (2000)

Writers are cultural brokers for the world of ideas. Our job is to share what we can, what we know.

Mary Pipher (b. 1947)
Writing to Change the World (2007)

Mr. C. had talent, but he couldn't spel. No man has a right to be a lit'rary man onless he knows how to spel. It is a pity that Chawcer, who had geneyus, was so unedicated. He's the wus speller I know of.

Artemus Ward (1834–67)
'Chaucer's Poems', *Artemus Ward in London* (1867)

Writer's block

If I'm stuck with a particular chapter or part of my book, I have been known to buy a return ticket, hop on a train and write.

Malorie Blackman (b. 1962)
Lucy Coats, 'Interview: Malorie Blackman', *Publishing Talk Magazine*, 2014

If you get to three chapters and are then stuck, you're not stuck, you're finished.

Fay Weldon (b. 1931)
Writers' & Artists' Yearbook (1999)

I don't believe in writer's block. [...] I think that the act of naming it as this thing called 'writer's block' actually exacerbates the problem and makes the writer feel powerless and the issue insurmountable.

Bernadine Evaristo (b. 1959)

'Bernardine Evaristo on the Illusion of Writer's Block', *Literary Hub*, 5 Nov 2019

I also like to remind myself of something my dad said in [response] to writers' block: 'Coal miners don't get coal miners' block.'

John Green (b. 1977)

Where I get my ideas, inspiration and general writing stuff, www.johngreenbooks.com

I often read, with amazement, of people who suffer from writer's block; I might enjoy a wee block, just to have time to catch my breath.

Robertson Davies (1913–95)

Elisabeth Sifton, 'Robertson Davies, The Art of Fiction No. 107', *The Paris Review*, Spring 1989

I LIKE TO WRITE WHEN I FEEL SPITEFUL: IT'S LIKE HAVING A GOOD SNEEZE.

D. H. Lawrence (1885–1930)
Letter to Lady Cynthia Asquith, 1913

I WRITE VERY SMALL SO I DON'T HAVE TO TURN THE PAGE AND FACE THE NEXT EMPTY ONE

Michael Morpurgo (b. 1943)
'Ten rules for writing fiction (Part two)', the *Guardian*, 20 February 2010

Indexes

Index of themes

Ability 7
Absorption 7
Achievement 8
Advice 9
Afflictions 9
Age 10
Agents 11
Alcohol 11
Ambition 12
Animals 13
Anxiety 14
Attention 15
Audience 16
Authenticity 18
Autobiography 19

Bad writing 23
Becoming a writer 23
Beginnings 24
Bestseller 25
Biography 26
Birds 27
Birth 28
Books 29
Bookshelf 31
Boredom 32
Brevity 32

Career 35
Characters 35
Children 36
Clarity 37
A Classic 38
Clichés 39
Comfort 40
Communication 41
Complaints 42
Conceit 42
Confidence 43
Conversation 44
Creativity 47
Criticism 48
Critics 50
Cynicism 52

Death 55
Discipline 56
Dislikes 57
Dogs 58
Dullness 58

Editing 61
Editors 62
Education 64
Emotion 65

Enjoyment 66
Equipment 66
Exercise 67

Fiction 69
Finishing 69
First draft 70
Formula 73
Friendship 74

Genius 77
Genre 78
A Good book 78
Grammar 79
Greatness 81

Hallucinations 83
Heroes 83
History 84
Humility 85
Humour 85

Ideas 89
Idleness 90
Ignorance 90
Imaginary worlds 91
Imagination 92

Insanity 94
Inspiration 97
Intellect 98
Isolation 99

Journalism 101
Judgement 102
Just write 102

Keep going 103

Language 107
Laziness 110
Libraries 110
Lies 112
Life 114
Lifeblood 115
Loss 115
Love and lust 116
Luck 117

Madness 119
Marriage 119
The Media 120
Medicine 121
Metaphor 121
Mightier than the
  sword 122
Misquotations 123
Money 123
Motive 125

Murder 126
Muse 127
Music 128

Narcissism 131
Night 131
Non-fiction 132
Novels 133

Obituaries 137
Originality 137

Passion 141
Pens and
  pencils 142
Perfection 143
Perspective 143
Pessimism 146
Plagiarism 146
Plays 148
Pleasure 149
Poetry 150
Poetry versus
  prose 152
Poets 155
Point of view 156
Power 157
Praise 157
Procrastination 158
Prose 159
Publication 160

Purpose 161

Quality 163
Quotations 164

Readable books 167
Reader 167
Reading 168
Rejection 172
Reputation 172
Research 173
Respect 174
Rewriting 175
Roads 176
Royalties 176
Rules 177

Satire 179
Science 180
Science fiction 180
Self-knowledge 181
Sentences 182
Sentimentality 184
Sex 184
Short stories 186
Soul 188
Speech 189
Speeches 190
Spontaneity 190
Struggle 191
Stupidity 192

Style 192
Submission 194
Success 194
Superiority 195

Talent 197
Taste 198
Technique 200
Time 201

Translation 202
Truth 204
Typewriter 205

Unhappiness 207
Unreadable 207

Vanity 208
Virtues and vices 209

Warfare 213
Wealth 213
Weather 214
Whispers 215
Wisdom 216
Wit 217
Words 218
Writers are ... 221
Writer's block 222

Index of quoted writers

Chinua Achebe 172, 201
André Aciman 116
Henry Adams 12
Joseph Addison 67
Chimamanda Ngozi Adichie 57, 93, 105, 174
Anna Akhmatova 150
Brian Aldiss 180, 181
Fred Allen 62
Isabel Allende 61
A. R. Ammons 175
Jean-Jaques Ampère 29
Maya Angelou 52, 92, 103, 200, 209
Matthew Arnold 48, 188
Joaquim Maria Machado de Assis 55
Diana Athill 61
Margaret Atwood 142, 167
W. H. Auden 18, 29, 66, 179, 214
Jane Austen 13, 191
Paul Auster 24
Alfred Austin 150
A. J. Ayer 183

Richard Bach 35
Francis Bacon 29, 41, 168, 170, 204, 216
Walter Bagehot 199
James Baldwin 145, 156
Arthur Balfour 168
Whitney Balliett 50

Toni Cade Bambara 133
Iain M. Banks 69
Théodore de Banville 150
Pat Barker 184
Julian Barnes 16, 204
Pío Baroja 35
J. M. Barrie 7, 159
Charles Baudelaire 158, 168, 174
Ann Beattie 215
Max Beerbohm 42, 98, 179, 208
Brendan Behan 137
Hilaire Belloc 137
Saul Bellow 9, 131
Robert Benchley 67
Walter Benjamin 158, 159
Alan Bennett 98, 148
Arnold Bennett 198
Edmund Clerihew Bentley 26
William Bernbach 41
John Betjeman 114
Mark Billingham 112, 167
Elizabeth Bishop 80, 96
Malorie Blackman 222
Quentin Blake 36
William Blake 192
Robert Bloch 35, 156
Louise Bogan 146
Jorge Luis Borges 83, 202, 208

Alain de Botton 164
Derek Brabazon 190
Ray Bradbury 70, 95, 172
John Braine 221
Gerald Brenan 39, 205
Vera Brittain 64
Charlotte Brontë 70, 143
Craig Brown 120
Rita Mae Brown 109, 198
Bill Bryson 38
Georg Büchner 84
Anthony Burgess 31
Edgar Rice Burroughs 105
John Burroughs 92
Robert Burton 119, 122, 147
Robert Burns 50
Samuel Butler 211

John Cage 150
Cai Qijiao 115
Italo Calvino 98, 109, 218
Patrick Campbell 101
Albert Camus 18, 77, 172
Elias Canetti 155
Nina Caplan 12
Truman Capote 23, 35, 189, 205
Thomas Carlyle 26, 32, 99, 157, 188
Raymond Carver 163
David Cecil 114
Bennett Cerf 10
Steph Cha 126

Raymond Chandler 79, 127
Anton Chekhov 50, 197
G. K. Chesterton 48, 53, 84, 101, 143
Chris Chibnall 200
Shirley Chisholm 52
Agatha Christie 90, 176
Winston Churchill 164
John Coate 41
Jean Cocteau 116, 154, 192, 221
Samuel Taylor Coleridge 81, 91, 153, 188
Samuel Coleridge-Taylor 145
Colette 56, 102
Cyril Connolly 63, 81, 101, 110, 193, 210
Shirley Conran 110
Bernard Cornwell 31, 163, 173, 177
Hart Crane 218
Quentin Crisp 19
Sarah Crossan 9

William Dalrymple 66, 97, 217
Guy Davenport 28, 128
Robertson Davies 216, 223
Clarence Shepard Day 70
Cecil Day-Lewis 154
John Denham 202
René Descartes 169, 211
Babette Deutsch 155
Philip K. Dick 181, 218
Emily Dickinson 77, 115
Joan Didion 132, 221
Annie Dillard 55, 56, 71, 102, 169, 191

Wentworth Dillon 20
Benjamin Disraeli 36, 133
E. L. Doctorow 133, 221
J. P. Donleavy 214
Emma Donoghue 57, 89
Thea Dorn 29
Roddy Doyle 89, 120
John Dryden 18
Lena Dunham 169
Geoff Dyer 171

Richard Eberhart 156
Umberto Eco 85, 150
Jennifer Egan 23, 67
George Eliot 144
T. S. Eliot 30, 62, 65, 110, 146
Havelock Ellis 19
Buchi Emecheta 184
Ralph Waldo Emerson 26, 64, 190, 197, 216
Anne Enright 142
Bernadine Evaristo 223

Clifton Fadiman 147
Faiz Ahmad Faiz 203
Nuruddin Farah 176
William Faulkner 71
Elena Ferrante 116
F. Scott Fitzgerald 11, 67, 83, 219
Janet Flanner 102
Gustave Flaubert 31, 137, 169, 180
Gillian Flynn 56

Richard Ford 116, 149
E. M. Forster 133
Gene Fowler 62
John Fowles 92
Benjamin Franklin 215
Jonathan Franzen 99, 124
Dawn French 201
Esther Freud 122
Robert Frost 65, 151, 202
Christopher Fry 107
Stephen Fry 9, 28
Margaret Fuller 51

Neil Gaiman 51, 142, 175
José Ortega y Gasset 122, 155
Roxane Gay 43
Maggie Gee 112
Stella Gibbons 101
Elizabeth Gilbert 12, 23, 47, 110, 127
Natalie Goldberg 47
Oliver Goldsmith 189
Maud Gonne 120
Maksim Gorky 37
Kenneth Grahame 209
Robert Graves 9, 10, 121, 175
John Green 15, 223
Graham Greene 83, 120, 185
John Grisham 197

Mark Haddon 44
Matt Haig 58, 71, 123, 182, 194

Lee Hall 141, 194
Philip Gilbert Hamerton 169
Mohsin Hamid 97
Isabella Hammad 94
Dashiell Hammett 193, 205
Christopher Hampton 58
Thomas Hardy 180
David Hare 28, 42
Deborah Harkness 91
Robert Harris 143
William Hazlitt 7, 90, 211, 216
Seamus Heaney 200
Heinrich Heine 220
Ernest Hemingway 24, 41, 94, 182, 214
Hans Werner Henze 7
David Hewson 47
Thomas Wentworth Higginson 172
Susan Hill 69, 147
Joseph Holloway 48
Oliver Wendell Holmes 138
Anthony Hope 217
Francis Hope 27
A. E. Housman 123, 149
Joseph Howe 119
Frank McKinney Hubbard 190
Ted Hughes 13
Zora Neale Hurston 174
Aldous Huxley 29, 43, 149

Richard Ingrams 160
Eugène Ionesco 146, 195

John Irving 135, 185
Christopher Isherwood 209

Henry James 32, 80, 104
P. D. James 23, 78, 126
William James 94
Randall Jarrell 96
Elizabeth Jennings 51
Jerome K. Jerome 43, 90
Samuel Johnson 59, 62, 112, 124, 142
Erica Jong 63, 102
Ben Jonson 155, 189
Michael Joseph 37
James Joyce 144

Franz Kafka 207
Jessica Francis Kane 194
Mary Karr 8
Alfred Kazin 38
John Keats 25, 44, 79, 81, 152, 188
Garrison Keillor 115
Helen Keller 75
A. L. Kennedy 33, 103, 117
John F. Kennedy 157
Ken Kesey 215
Ralph Keyes 14
Søren Kierkegaard 207
Jamaica Kincaid 113
Rudyard Kipling 137
Arthur Koestler 161
Dean Koontz 73

Karl Kraus 32, 42, 107, 131, 203
Milan Kundera 192
R. O. Kwon 11

R. D. Laing 29
Charles Lamb 58, 99
Anne Lamott 71, 160
Philip Larkin 20, 73, 121, 139, 185, 195
D. H. Lawrence 50, 164, 190, 195, 224
Ursula K. Le Guin 78, 92, 176, 177
Stephen Leacock 198
Fran Lebowitz 46
J. Robert Lennon 201
Elmore Leonard 214
C. S. Lewis 37
Wyndham Lewis 89
Georg Christoph Lichtenberg 5
Mario Vargas Llosa 113
David Lodge 167
Jack London 97
Alice Lee Longworth 44
Federico García Lorca 28
Audre Lorde 164
H. P. Lovecraft 132
Lu Xun 125

Thomas Babington Macaulay 13, 119
Rose Macaulay 56, 152
Norman Mailer 184
Osip Mandelstam 121
Alberto Manguel 170, 203

Katherine Mansfield 103
Hilary Mantel 124
Mao Zedong 170
Walter de la Mare 221
Gabriel García Márquez 135
George R. R. Martin 66
Groucho Marx 58, 111, 159
W. Somerset Maugham 10, 53, 159, 163, 184
John McPhee 96
H. L. Mencken 53, 128, 151, 217
W. S. Merwin 113
John Stuart Mill 138
Henry Miller 129, 157
Madeline Miller 83
A. A. Milne 16, 148
John Milton 79, 115
David Mitchell 7
G. E. Mitton 117
Wilson Mizner 51, 147
Ferenc Molnár 149
Harriet Monroe 152
Montesquieu 121
Brian Moore 173
Lorrie Moore 135
Caitlin Moran 66, 213
Paul Morand 208
Thomas More 153
Christopher Darlington Morley 44, 119
Robert Morley 44
Michael Morpurgo 224

Toni Morrison 48, 52, 90, 108, 134
Andrew Motion 132
Malcolm Muggeridge 213
Max Müller 19
Alice Munro 175
Haruki Murakami 220
Iris Murdoch 85, 117

Vladimir Nabokov 39, 67, 84, 192,
  202
V. S. Naipaul 119
Gerard de Naval 39
Patrick Ness 89
Friedrich Wilhelm Nietzsche 14
Anaïs Nin 141
Lawrence Norfolk 11
Mary Norris 220

Joyce Carol Oates 53, 220
Téa Obreht 160
Sean O'Casey 14
Flannery O'Connor 135, 161, 170
Frank O'Connor 186
Ben Okri 186
Charles Olson 168
Joe Orton 199
George Orwell 38, 125, 159
Charles Osbourne 116
John Osborne 17, 195
Wilfred Owen 204, 213

Amos Oz 13, 146
Cynthia Ozick 35

Marcel Pagnol 181
Dorothy Parker 21, 124, 173, 207
Adele Parks 8, 24, 99, 127
Blaise Pascal 25
Ann Patchett 74
Hesketh Pearson 123
S. J. Perelman 124
Jodi Picoult 61
Harold Pinter 148
Mary Pipher 107, 222
Sylvia Plath 47, 156
Edgar Allan Poe 180
Emily Post 45
Beatrix Potter 25, 138
Ezra Pound 128, 167, 200
Terry Pratchett 72, 139, 144
J. B. Priestley 42, 52, 77, 173
V. S. Pritchett 134
E. Annie Proulx 36
Philip Pullman 55

Salvatore Quasimodo 40
Thomas De Quincey 141, 157

Walter Alexander Raleigh 1
Charles Reade 65
Wilhelm Reich 186

Jules Renard 37, 189, 197, 214
Ruth Rendell 86
Adrienne Rich 49
Mordecai Richler 210
Rainer Maria Rilke 49
Alain Robbe-Grillet 193
Samuel Rogers 160
Franklin D. Roosevelt 122
Philip Roth 56, 175
John Ruskin 26, 78, 167
Bertrand Russell 27, 108, 125, 185

Herbert Samuel 112
Carl Sandburg 8
Ken Saro-Wiwa 198
Jean-Paul Sartre 18, 93, 191
Marjane Satrapi 131
Ben Schott 80, 187
C. P. Scott 120
Elif Shafak 24, 103
Ntozake Shange 170
Karl Shapiro 182
George Bernard Shaw 179, 185
John Sheffield 163
Percy Bysshe Shelley 40
Sam Shepard 73
Robert E. Sherwood 179
Georges Simenon 207
Charles Simic 14
Neil Simon 10

Edith Sitwell 152
Jane Smiley 72
Ali Smith 203
Logan Pearsall Smith 25, 169, 189, 215
Stevie Smith 40
Sydney Smith 31, 45, 91, 217
Zadie Smith 144, 201
Song Lin 107
Susan Sontag 15, 85, 127
Robert Southey 45
Lord Philip Stanhope 9, 15
Lincoln Steffens 192
Gertrude Stein 183, 205
John Steinbeck 59, 105, 158, 183
George Steiner 31, 108
Wallace Stevens 77, 93, 94, 155
Adlai Stevenson 62
Robert Stevenson 148
Robert Louis Stevenson 113, 114
Tom Stoppard 45
Emma Straub 125
Simeon Strunsky 123
Anne Sullivan 108
Jonathan Swift 193
Robert Sylvester 126
J. M. Synge 93

Donna Tartt 143
Twyla Tharp 138
Angie Thomas 65

Dylan Thomas 158, 208
Henry David Thoreau 32, 183
James Thurber 49, 87
Colm Tóibín 12, 27, 165
J. R. R. Tolkien 57
Sophia Tolstoy 209
P. L. Travers 97
Rose Tremain 21, 25, 177
Lionel Trilling 215
Anthony Trollope 69
Joanna Trollope 19, 85, 216
Martin Farquhar Tupper 74
Mark Twain 61, 95, 137, 190
Kenneth Tynan 52

Miguel de Unamuno y Jugo 203
Stanley Unwin 15
John Updike 49, 101
Peter Ustinov 8

Paul Valéry 69, 128
Gore Vidal 18, 81, 131, 133
John Vorster 49

John Wain 152
Alice Walker 37, 91, 114, 187
David Foster Wallace 40
Phoebe Waller-Bridge 16
Artemus Ward 222

Evelyn Waugh 32, 105, 219
Beatrice Webb 43
Simone Weil 93
Fay Weldon 161, 222
H. G. Wells 141, 213
John Wesley 38
Rebecca West 27
Edith Wharton 39, 73
E. B. White 80, 186
Patrick White 28
A. N. Whitehead 138
Katharine Whitehorn 45
Walt Whitman 19
Oscar Wilde 17, 57
Alan D. Williams 64
Joy Williams 74, 193
Tennessee Williams 55
William Carlos Williams 204
August Wilson 16, 174
Jeanette Winterson 23, 158, 182
P. G. Wodehouse 84, 132
Tom Wolfe 46, 114
Meg Wolitzer 36
Virginia Woolf 12, 87, 153
Alexander Woollcott 50, 98
William Wordsworth 65, 153
Lois Wyse 75

W. B. Yeats 191